Dear reader:

The fifth-century church father, Augustine, once said that the Bible is shallow enough for a lamb to wade in but deep enough for an elephant to drown in. With a similar aim, the AGO subscription series strives to provide profound and insightful spiritual information to people at all levels of faith. This means solid scholarship, careful exegesis, and colorful presentation of Biblical truths consumable by both the young and old in Christ.

The book you are holding in your hands does exactly that. Stephen Davey is especially adept at presenting scholarly biblical truths in bright and memorable ways. Through exhaustive research and careful organization, his messages flow clearly and logically to practical application. Along the way, he illustrates God's truths with unforgettable colorations. When these messages are compiled into commentary form, as with this work, the logical flow is even more pronounced.

I promise readers of this volume a treat. It is chock-full of clear scriptural truths explained and expanded by Stephen's masterful touch. You will not only learn, you will remember. You will not only gain, you will grow. And even though the book of Esther is famous for not directly mentioning God, you will stand in awe at His mighty work in the life of one young Jewish woman and the love with which He preserves His people.

Sincerely,

Chris Brady

Stephen Davey

WISDOM COMMENTARY SERIES

ESTHER

CHARITY HOUSE
PUBLISHERS

Wisdom Commentary Series: Esther

Author: Stephen Davey
Editorial Team: Lalanne Barber, J. Seth Davey
Cover Design and Body Layout: Grace Gourley
Photo of Stephen: Sam Gray Portraits, Raleigh, NC (samgrayportraits.com)
ISBN 978 0 9776641 3 9

Published by Charity House Publishers

Charity House Publishers, Inc.
2201 Candun Street
Suite 103
Apex, NC 27523-6412
USA

*With loving gratitude to my mother Yvonne Davey,
who raised her four sons to think first of Christ and His Word;
who instilled in us the truth—both by her words and her life—
that greatness is measured in terms of that little plaque
which hung over our kitchen door:
"Only one life, 'twill soon be past;
Only what's done for Christ will last."*

CONTENTS

Now it took place in the days of Ahasuerus, the Ahasuerus who reigned from India to Ethiopia over 127 provinces, ²in those days as King Ahasuerus sat on his royal throne which was in Susa the capital, ³in the third year of his reign, he gave a banquet for all his princes and attendants, the army officers of Persia and Media, the nobles, and the princes of his provinces being in his presence. ⁴And he displayed the riches of his royal glory and the splendor of his great majesty for many days, 180 days.

–Esther 1:1-4

CHAPTER ONE

JUST ABOVE THE ROYAL THRONE

Esther 1:1-4

THE QUESTION OF THE AGES

Ravi Zacharias, a well-known apologist, remarked that in all his lectures and debates at prestigious universities such as Princeton and Oxford, he has never once defended the existence of God without being questioned about the problem of evil.

The predicament of suffering and evil is a universal phenomenon, and believers and unbelievers alike struggle with the question of why God allows it.

The difference, however, is that suffering takes unbelievers farther from a belief in an involved, powerful, caring God, while suffering brings Christians closer to Him.

Unbelievers use the question of evil to reject God and come up with their own answers.

Theologians call this issue theodicy (Greek *theo* - "God"; Greek *dicy* or *dike* - "justice").

In other words, theodicy grapples with the question of how a sovereign, just God can allow injustice to go seemingly unchecked.

It is this issue of unchecked evil that leads to a secular view that God is either an exaggerated concept, or He doesn't exist at all.

The secular conclusion is based on these four arguments:

1. Evil and suffering exist in the world.

2. If God were all-powerful, He *could* prevent evil and suffering.

3. If God were all-loving, He would *want* to prevent evil and suffering.

4. Therefore, since evil and suffering still exist in the world, either God is not powerful enough to stop it, not loving enough to stop it, or He merely doesn't exist.

This argument poses a logical and theological problem for the Christian. The Bible clearly tells us that:

- God is both all-powerful and all-loving. He is the God of gods and the Lord of lords, mighty and awesome *(Deuteronomy 10:17)*.

- He works all things to the conformity of His will *(Ephesians 1:11)*.

- He is compassionate, gracious, and abounding in love *(Psalm 103:8)*.[1]

The Bible is unapologetic in its description of God.

So how do we reconcile the Bible with current events? The world is full of evil . . . is God asleep? Is He absent? Is He powerless to intervene? Worse yet, does He not even care?

Before we answer these questions, it's important to first define what we mean by evil. When people speak about evil, they are referring to two different categories of evil:

1. **moral evil** – Under this category fall murder, rape, theft, political oppression, physical abuse, sex trafficking, terrorist attacks, genocide, and poverty due to corruption, among other things.

2. **natural evil** – This is identified by theologians as diseases and epidemics, brutality in the animal kingdom, and disasters caused by forces of nature that ravish entire nations, causing drought and famine.

No one doubts that the world is filled with both moral and natural evil.

One author wrote that if we could see just a fraction of the evil and suffering in the world going on at any given moment, we would collapse from the horror of it all.

Another said that the history of the human race is nothing less than the history of evil and suffering.

We all know we're living in a messed-up world. But what we can't quite figure out is why God is allowing it to stay that way. Every time disaster strikes, people stop and ask the same old question they've been asking for centuries: **"Where is God?"**

After the recent Indian Ocean earthquake and tsunami, when hundreds of thousands died and entire cities were washed off the map, a United Nations spokesman said that in terms of the areas affected—from Indonesia to Kenya—this was the greatest natural catastrophe in the world's history. The carnage was inconceivable.

An English newspaper summed up the thinking of many when one of its journalists declared, "Those with religious beliefs are right to consider this national disaster a test of their faith. Does it not seem that if there is a God, He is now malicious or mad or dead?"[2]

Many Americans remember where they were on September 11, 2001, when the Twin Towers of the World Trade Center collapsed in seconds.

I was in Chennai, India, and I'll never forget sitting in the home of the college president, watching television coverage of the two airplanes that flew into the towers. Office equipment, paper, and body parts rained down on the surrounding streets, as one author put it, "like a ticker tape parade."

Ninety minutes later the towers collapsed, causing the deaths of nearly 3,000 men, women, and children. It was the bloodiest day in our nation's history since the Civil War.

"History will never be the same again,"[3] quoted one newspaper and, thus far, it has proven so. But before you reach the conclusion that God is malicious, insane, or dead—which many Americans concluded that fateful day—you should ask yourself a couple important questions.

THE LOGICAL ARGUMENT

Why does human suffering bother us anyway? And if Oxford professor Peter Atkins is right to call mankind "a bit of slime on a planet," why should we concern ourselves with *anybody*?

The truth is there is something inherent in our human consciousness which causes us to care for loved ones, feed the hungry, declare the injustice of social classes, and stand against racism. We can deny with our mouths there is such a thing as a Moral Lawgiver, but our actions give us away.

Here's the point: **moral evil doesn't rule out God**. The very fact that we can identify something as morally wrong implies that there is a Moral Lawgiver who created our conscience.

This moral compass which is hard-wired in all of us is also *the* distinctive that separates us from the animal kingdom.

My dog Pixie is classic evidence of this.

When Pixie's lying out in the backyard watching hummingbirds drink from the feeders my wife puts up in the summer, she isn't lying there wondering about all the other hummingbirds in the world that might be dying of thirst.

She never comes up on the deck where Marsha and I like to sit, wanting to see if we're having a good day. She doesn't even care if we're getting along as a married couple. She just wants to know if there's anything to eat.

She barks her head off at the neighbor's dog that comes over to sniff around, never thinking for a moment that her behavior isn't good for her testimony.

She doesn't care about her testimony . . . she doesn't have one.

Humans, on the other hand, created in God's image, have an innate sense of right and wrong.

Why do we go out of our way to help someone? Why do we love our family and make sacrifices for them? Why do we treat people with justice, fairness, and compassion, and *expect* the same treatment in return?

It's because we have a moral law written on our heart. As soon as we look at something and objectively label it good or evil, we reveal there is something outside ourselves—something *beyond* us.

That *Something* is God.

Scripture tells us that God has stamped His image on humanity and given us the ability to distinguish between good and evil, fairness and partiality, love and hatred.

If we're just slime on the planet or an accident in some backwater pond, we wouldn't care about someone else's suffering any more than my dog cares about hummingbirds.

So the answer to the logical question of why we have a problem with evil is that God has placed that sense of right and wrong within us.

THE THEOLOGICAL ARGUMENT

What does the Bible say about evil and its purpose? If the British philosopher and evolutionist Bertrand Russell was correct in dismissing man as "a curious accident," why should it matter in the least whether people die suddenly or slowly . . . peacefully or painfully?

In other words, how does Scripture reconcile the issue of theodicy (the existence of God with the existence of evil)?

The Apostle Paul gives us some insight into that question in *Romans 5:12*, when he makes it clear that death, pain, disease, and calamity came as a result of sin. The sin of our first parents Adam and Eve polluted the stream of human existence that has infected every human being since.

For all have sinned and fall short of the glory of God (Romans 3:23).

Paul writes that the entire world system, including nature itself, fell as a result of that original sin. Even the universe groans for the day of redemption, according to *Romans 8:22*.

The Bible also tells us that our mysterious God, whose ways are far beyond our ways and whose thoughts are much higher than our thoughts, is actually sovereign over evil:

- He is never surprised by sin.
- His plans are never counteracted by corruption.
- His will is never restricted by rebellion.
- He is not inhibited by iniquity.

While He already knew, before time began, every evil deed that would take place, He works in spite of them to accomplish His own wise and holy purposes.[4]

Ultimately, God is able to make all things—including the fruits of all the evil of all time—work to the fulfillment of His sovereign plan *(Romans 8:28-29; Ephesians 1:11)*.

Are we suggesting that God actually plans for people to endure suffering and pain, hatred and cruelty, injustice and murder? Are we saying that God is actually the One orchestrating those things in a person's life?

That's *exactly* what we're saying.

But that's not *all* we're saying.

THE GREATEST ARGUMENT

Before time began, the **Triune God decided that Jesus Christ would suffer the wrath of both man and God in order to redeem men from their sins.**

Anyone who claims that God must be a malicious God to allow suffering and pain, hatred and cruelty to work toward the accomplishment of His will is either overlooking or simply misunderstanding that same critical component of the Christian message: the crucifixion of Jesus Christ.

The spiritual, physical, and emotional anguish Jesus was made to endure was not an accident. It was planned—on purpose, too.

That's why the prophets could describe the suffering of the Messiah in *Isaiah 53* and *Psalm 22* with perfect precision centuries *before* Christ was born.

Yes, Pilate and the Jewish people made immoral and corrupt decisions of their own accord, of which they would be responsible; God's sovereignty doesn't erase man's responsibility.

But behind the scenes of the crucifixion, God was pulling the strings to accomplish the plan He had ordained before the world began *(Revelation 13:8)*.

The Apostle Peter understood this clearly, because when he preached to the Jewish people on the day of Pentecost, he didn't say, "Now look what you've done . . . you've ruined everything . . . you crucified the true Messiah. What are we going to do now?"

Instead, Peter preached one of the most powerful statements relating to theodicy that you will find in Scripture. He said,

> *"This Man* [Jesus the Nazarene] *delivered up by the predetermined plan and foreknowledge of God, you nailed to a cross by the hands of godless men and put Him to death"* (Acts 2:23).

In other words, Peter was telling the Jews that something bigger was at work behind their decision. Someone greater than Pilate was in charge.

God knew it would happen. He ordained it. It happened according to His *predetermined plan.* That's why Jesus' last words "It is finished!" were not a cry of failure but a cry of fulfillment.

THE PERSONAL ARGUMENT

Death is certain. Evil came into the world through the fall of man, and Jesus dealt with evil at the cross. But that's not the end of the story. Scripture also tells us of a day when God will right all the wrongs humans have done.

When a tower in Jerusalem suddenly toppled over, crushing 18 people to death, those around Jesus asked Him why innocent people died.

In His response found in Luke's Gospel, Jesus shifted the focus of the question away from why those specific people died and placed the emphasis on the question of why *everyone* dies. Death is always tragic. The problem isn't that it touches someone suddenly but, rather, that it touches all of us inevitably.

Death came about through evil—i.e., man's sin—so Jesus asked His audience whether they were ready to die and face the Judge.

John Blanchard writes:

> There is a coming day when God will make a universal adjustment. Perfect justice will be dispensed. The wicked will no longer prosper and the righteous will no longer suffer and the problem of evil will be fully and finally settled beyond all doubt and dispute.[5]

When you read the headlines that speak of natural disasters and moral acts of evil, take them as reminders that life is brief and fragile. But God is sovereign even over death, and He will one day make all things right and new. That being said, you might still be thinking to yourself, "Okay, but why doesn't God just eradicate all the evil in the world in the meantime?"

I'll give you at least one good reason: if God eradicated all the evil in the world, that would mean He would have to eradicate *you . . . and me.*

When would you like Him to start?

The point is God understands the problem of evil more than any one of us does. If anyone knew what it meant to suffer, it was God's Son. If anyone knew what it meant to be forsaken and misunderstood, it was Jesus. If anyone had a right to call life unfair, it was our Lord. That is why, though we may never get an answer to the problem of evil in this life, we confidently serve a God who understands. And that should give us comfort.

THE DIVINE ANSWER TO THE QUESTION

The cross is the answer to theodicy. Scripture makes it clear that God is rich in mercy. Because of His grace and love He gives mankind opportunity after opportunity to believe in Him . . . to accept Him . . . to love Him . . . to come to the cross of Christ and see the arms of Justice bearing our injustice.

While it marked the greatest act of human *injustice* in history, it also marked the greatest act of divine *justice* in history. The plans of sinful man and a sovereign God converged at the cross.

God was actually ordering the chaos and the corruption to fulfill His plan of redemption. God was in control.

That truth is easy to preach, but I admit it isn't easy to understand. It's even harder to live out, isn't it?

It's one thing to believe that God is sovereign over the chaos of life—it's another thing to believe He's sovereign over the chaos in *our* life.

Yet, that's one of the wonderful and mysterious truths about God's sovereignty. Even when it doesn't *seem* like He's in control, He is. Even when towers crumble to the ground and nations are left in uproar, God is on His throne. Even when tsunamis wipe out thousands of unsuspecting people, God is still merciful. Even in the drudgery of our day-to-day lives, God has a purpose.

When we don't see His hand, when we don't hear His voice, when we can't make sense of the tumult around us . . . God is working all things out for His glory *and* for our good.

And that's the truth we find profoundly displayed in the Book of Esther. That's why we're going to dive into this Old Testament drama with excitement and expectation because, although God's name is never mentioned throughout the entire story, we will witness His presence on every page.

A DRAMA OF GOOD VS. EVIL

The Book of Esther, perhaps more so than any other book in Scripture, reminds us that a faithful God is in control . . . even when God seems absent from the drama of history, He is still the main character.

So let's shift our attention from the general questions about evil and God's providence, and watch how they play out in the real-life drama of Esther.

At the time Esther's story begins, the Jews were struggling with their own questions of evil. They had been in bondage for hundreds of years because of their lack of obedience to God. Their God, Who had for so long spoken to His people through the kings and prophets, was now silent.

During this time of silence, the Jews had been taken into captivity. Those who lived in Jerusalem had been carried away by the Babylonian king Nebuchadnezzar—the same king responsible for destroying the city's walls and temple, pillaging, plundering, and making off with their treasures.

Fifty years later, Cyrus conquered Babylon when his soldiers diverted the water of the Euphrates River that ran through the capital city and he literally waded underneath the iron spikes of the wall and into the city.

Just before Cyrus showed up with his army, Nebuchadnezzar's son Belshazzar was having a drunken orgy in his palace. The Bible records that a hand suddenly appeared and began writing on the wall letters that no one could understand. Needless to say, that ruined the party.

They called the prophet Daniel out of retirement so he could read the words on the wall and interpret the message to Belshazzar: effectively, "You're toast!"

And Daniel's interpretation came true that very night. Belshazzar was killed and the Persian kingdom replaced the kingdom of Babylon. Cyrus the Great was now ruler of the known world.

God was orchestrating all of this. He moved in Cyrus' heart to show mercy to the Jewish people and allow them to return home for the next few decades. Sadly, many refused. They had become so entrenched in the Persian culture around them that they no longer had any desire to return to Jerusalem.

Many of them had simply become *Persianized*—fully rooted in the culture of the kingdom around them.

And by now, the promises of God seemed far-fetched. The Jews of Esther's day were the grandchildren of those who were exiled. Their sense of nationalism was weak because they had never once stepped foot into Jerusalem.

In their minds, God belonged in Jerusalem. He was a relic of the past—as broken as the city that once bore His name.

Persia was the "new" Jerusalem.

That's why the Book of Esther never mentions Jerusalem or the Temple or the Law or the Abrahamic Covenant or the Passover or Jehovah. The king's name is written 190 times in 167 verses. God's name is not mentioned at all.[6]

So the question that faces us even at the outset of this story is not whether God will prove sovereign over His people in Jerusalem, but whether He will prove sovereign over His people in *Persia*. It seems natural that God will lead and direct those who chose to return home . . . but will He lead and direct those who didn't?

Yes. We'll be reminded throughout this story that even when God's people forget Him, He doesn't forget them.

THE ONE WHO SAT ON THE THRONE

In the opening lines of this drama, we're introduced immediately to Cyrus' grandson Ahasuerus.

Now it took place in the days of Ahasuerus, the Ahasuerus who reigned from India to Ethiopia over 127 provinces (Esther 1:1).

Ahasuerus was not the king's proper name, however. It was just his kingly, formal title—like Pharaoh to the Egyptians or Caesar to the Romans. It meant "Chief of rulers."

The king's real name was Xerxes, "Sovereign over men"[7] or "Hero of heroes."[8] Scripture always refers to the king by his title, however, so that's how we'll refer to him throughout this study.

As the Book of Esther opens, we are struck by the power and influence of this king, even in the first line of this story. The point is obvious to the reader . . . Ahasuerus is in charge.

One inscription was discovered where the king wrote this of himself: "I am Xerxes, the great king, the only king, the king of this entire earth, far and near."[9]

Herodotus, a Greek historian who lived just after the Persian Empire was defeated, wrote that Xerxes was the tallest and most handsome of the Persian kings, and he was ambitious, ruthless, and jealous.[10] Proof of his ruthlessness is found in the war stories collected by Herodotus:

A man named Pythius offered Ahasuerus an enormous amount of money in support of his military expedition against Greece. Ahasuerus, moved by this man's loyalty, returned the gift and sent presents back to Pythius. However, when Pythius asked Ahasuerus to allow his oldest son to remain home from the war, the king, enraged by the request, ordered the son to be cut into two pieces and had the army march between them on their way to battle.

During his expedition against Greece—the same where he and more than 100,000 soldiers were held off for seven days by Leonidus and 300 brave Spartans at the battle of Thermopylae—Ahasuerus attempted to build two bridges across a river to accommodate his huge army. Although they were successfully built, a storm rose up and destroyed the bridges overnight. Furious and delusional, the king had a soldier beat the river with a whip 300 times while other soldiers shouted and cursed at the water. He also ordered that a pair of shackles be thrown into the river to symbolize his sovereignty over the waters, even though he had failed to cross it. As final proof of his absolute dominance of all things, he then had the bridge engineers beheaded.[11]

On another occasion, he travelled back to Susa and wintered in the city of Sardis where he tried to seduce his sister-in-law. She refused his advances and, as a result, he later had her and her husband (his own brother) tortured to death.[12]

This is the bleak portrait of a king who will take center stage in the story of Esther. Haughty, angry, merciless—Xerxes wanted control over everything. And from the looks of it . . . he had it.

His kingdom included modern-day Turkey, Iraq, Iran, Pakistan, Jordan, Lebanon, Israel, Egypt, Sudan, Libya, and Arabia.

Herodotus records that Xerxes' riches were legendary. In fact, the tribute he received from the subjugated nations around him totaled more than 700 tons of gold and silver annually.[13]

Millions of people from diverse cultures, religions, and ethnicities gave their allegiance to this king. He was known as the Great King—the King of kings . . . the only king over all the earth.[14]

He was seated in the great citadel at Susa, the palace where his own son would one day be served by Nehemiah. This is the same citadel where Daniel was buried. Several times in the opening verses of Esther we're told that Ahasuerus reigned and he was sitting on his throne.

He seemed to be the preeminent mover and shaker in the kingdom of Persia. But behind the scenes, he was just a pawn in the hands of the real Mover and Shaker of the kingdom.

THE SHADOW ABOVE THE THRONE

If you get nothing else out of this study, get this: **Even when God is invisible, He is still invincible.**

World events, whether good or evil, are nothing more than the choreography of our Creator Who will bring His will to perfect completion. You may not understand the movements, but you can trust the Creator of them.

In ***Esther 1*** it looks like Ahasuerus is the man with the power over the greatest kingdom on the planet. He is seated on his throne in the palace at Susa. But if you look a little closer, you'll see the shadow of Providence hovering just above that royal throne.

God may remain hidden . . . but He is not absent.

He may be invisible . . . but He is infallible.

He may be quiet . . . but He has undiminished control.

He may be disregarded . . . but His will is never frustrated.

He may be unnoticed . . . but He remains unconquerable.

"For His dominion is an everlasting dominion, and His kingdom endures from generation to generation . . . He does according to His will in the host of heaven, and among the inhabitants of the earth; and no one can ward off His hand or say to Him, 'What have You done?'" (Daniel 4:34*b*-35).

Whatever the LORD pleases, He does, in heaven and in earth, in the seas and in all deep places (Psalm 135:6).

The Book of Esther was not given to us to enamor us with Esther; it was given to enamor us with God. We're given the inside story *not* so we will say, "Oh, look how clever Esther and Mordecai were." We're given the inside story so we can say, "Look how wise God is."

It is my prayerful intention and desire that as we move through this short book on the drama of Esther, you will not find yourself loving her more but, rather, you'll find yourself loving Him more.

God is the Author of this story.

He is the Hero of the drama.

He is the King . . . behind the "seen."

³[I]n the third year of his reign, he gave a banquet for all his princes and attendants, the army officers of Persia and Media, the nobles, and the princes of his provinces being in his presence. ⁴And he displayed the riches of his royal glory and the splendor of his great majesty for many days, 180 days. ⁵And when these days were completed, the king gave a banquet lasting seven days for all the people who were present in Susa the capital, from the greatest to the least, in the court of the garden of the king's palace. ⁶There were hangings of fine white and violet linen held by cords of fine purple linen on silver rings and marble columns, and couches of gold and silver on a mosaic pavement of porphyry, marble, mother-of-pearl, and precious stones. ⁷Drinks were served in golden vessels of various kinds, and the royal wine was plentiful according to the king's bounty. ⁸And the drinking was done according to the law, there was no compulsion, for so the king had given orders to each official of his household that he should do according to the desires of each person. ⁹Queen Vashti also gave a banquet for the women in the palace which belonged to King Ahasuerus. ¹⁰On the seventh day, when the heart

(Continued on next page)

(Continued)

of the king was merry with wine, he commanded Mehuman, Biztha, Harbona, Bigtha, Abagtha, Zethar, and Carkas, the seven eunuchs who served in the presence of King Ahasuerus, ¹¹to bring Queen Vashti before the king with her royal crown in order to display her beauty to the people and the princes, for she was beautiful. ¹²But Queen Vashti refused to come at the king's command delivered by the eunuchs. Then the king became very angry and his wrath burned within him. ¹³Then the king said to the wise men who understood the times—for it was the custom of the king so to speak before all who knew law and justice, ¹⁴and were close to him: Carshena, Shethar, Admatha, Tarshish, Meres, Marsena, and Memucan, the seven princes of Persia and Media who had access to the king's presence and sat in the first place in the kingdom—¹⁵"According to law, what is to be done with Queen Vashti, because she did not obey the command of King Ahasuerus delivered by the eunuchs?" ¹⁶And in the presence of the king and the princes, Memucan said, "Queen Vashti has wronged not only the king but also all the princes, and all the peoples who are in all the provinces of King Ahasuerus. ¹⁷For the queen's conduct will become known to all the women causing them to look with contempt on their husbands by saying, 'King Ahasuerus commanded Queen Vashti to be brought in to his presence, but she did not come.' ¹⁸And this day the ladies of Persia and Media who have heard of the queen's conduct will speak in the same way to all the king's princes, and there will be plenty of contempt and anger. ¹⁹If it pleases the king, let a royal edict be issued by him and let it be written in the laws of Persia and Media so that it cannot be repealed, that Vashti should come no more into the presence of King Ahasuerus, and let the king give her royal position to another who is more worthy than she. ²⁰And when the king's edict which he shall make is heard throughout all his kingdom, great as it is, then all women will give honor to their husbands, great and small." ²¹And this word pleased the king and the princes, and the king did as Memucan proposed. ²²So he sent letters to all the king's provinces, to each province according to its script and to every people according to their language, that every man should be the master in his own house and the one who speaks in the language of his own people.

–Esther 1:3-22

CHAPTER TWO

THE CURTAIN RISES

Esther 1:3-22

A LIMITED RECORD

For many centuries the Book of Esther caused a great deal of heartburn in the Church, mostly owing to the fact that God is never mentioned once throughout its entirety.

The Reformer Martin Luther didn't like the book because it included what he called "too many heathen unnaturalities." Another Reformer John Calvin never preached one sermon from it and didn't include the book in his commentaries.

For the first 700 years of church history, not one commentary was produced on the Book of Esther.[1]

The Jewish people, on the other hand, revered the book. Moses Maimonides, a famous twelfth-century Jewish doctor and teacher, considered Esther equal with the first five books of the Old Testament (the Books of Moses) in spite of the fact that neither Esther nor Mordecai ever mentioned God's law once.

The Jews did, however, try to modify the book. They composed 107 additional verses, including prayers by Mordecai and Esther, which they slotted neatly into the pages of the Septuagint (the Greek translation of the Book of Esther).[2] It was their attempt to make Esther a little more palatable. They thought they would help God out by tying up some of those loose ends.

While those 107 additions were later endorsed by the Catholic Church in the sixteenth century, Protestant scholars chose to accept the book as it was first penned by Ezra (the most likely author) and his associates.

The rough edges were left intact. The "heathen unnaturalities" and the missing prayers or mention of God remained unedited. This is the point of the book—which is one of the primary lessons God wants us to learn: namely, that He is faithful even when His people are not.

Although the Book of Esther is never quoted in the New Testament, neither is Ezra nor Nehemiah. But there are some who see a reference to Esther in *Hebrews 11:34*: the people of God, we're told, escaped the edge of the sword.

Still, the Book of Esther has become one of the greatest revelations of the providence of God in all Scripture. The absence of God's name may very well be deliberate. From beginning to end, the story so wonderfully reveals that even when God is invisible, He is still involved. Even in the shadows, we discover He is the Shadow Sovereign.

As J. Vernon McGee said, "Providence is the hand of God in the glove of history."[3] And in the drama of Esther, we see His hand at work on every page.

As we approach an exposition of this book, imagine you are seeing it played out onstage. I want you to think of Esther as a major dramatic production with sets, lights, and larger-than-life characters.

My wife and I enjoy attending plays from time to time. The last one we saw together was our daughter's Senior High play at Wake Christian Academy. Charity landed a role in the production *Little Orphan Annie*. But of all the characters she *could* have played, she took on the role of the rather unsanctified, sassy, brazen young woman who posed as Annie's long-lost mother, deceiving everyone and stealing the reward.

As the curtain rose, my younger daughter came out in saucy style, smacking her gum and speaking with a New York accent, while she and her boyfriend planned their deception. People came up to me afterward and said, "We've never seen Charity like that before." I had one guy say, "Wow, what a convincing acting job." to which I replied, "A little too convincing . . . when she gets home, I'm putting her on restriction!"

Maybe you've attended a play, and the usher handed you a playbill as you entered the theatre.

- You took time to look over the introduction.
- You read the bio of the actors and the characters they were portraying.
- You scanned the summary of each scene to get a feel for the setting of the action.

Then the houselights went down, the curtain rose, and you were awed by the sets and costumes. You put your playbill away, settled back in your seat, and took in the action as it began to unfold on the stage.

That's exactly what happens here in Act I, Scene I of this divine drama. As the curtain rises, the setting reveals an incredibly lavish reception taking place for all the powerful people in the kingdom of Persia.

A LAVISH RECEPTION

[I]n the third year of his reign he gave a banquet for all his princes and attendants, the army officers of Persia and Media, the nobles, and the princes of his provinces being in his presence. And he displayed the riches of his royal glory and the splendor of his great majesty for many days, 180 days (Esther 1:3-4).

To say this king was rich would be a vast understatement. He was made out of money. In fact, when Alexander the Great arrived in Persia 200 years later, he was mesmerized not only by the beauty of the palace at Susa but the discovery of more than a thousand tons of gold bullion and 270 tons of gold coins.[4]

Ahasuerus—better known as Xerxes—had money to burn. He was able to feed his guests from all around the kingdom for 180 days. If you're doing the math, that's six months.

Paying for that lavish banquet wasn't nearly as difficult for him as it was for you to pay for your daughter's wedding reception.

Imagine throwing a wedding reception for hundreds of people that lasted half a year. No way. Both of my daughters have been told that Smithfield's Barbecue has everything they need. I think it's settled—at least, for now.

Regardless of what was on the menu there at the king's reception, you need to know that this elaborate banquet wasn't just a dinner party. It was part of the Great War Council of 483 B.C., where Ahasuerus' main goal was to convince his leaders to invade the Grecian empire. Greece and Persia were the two great superpowers of the world at that time.

This truly was the Banquet of the Century, and anybody who was *anybody* got an invitation. Ahasuerus had gathered all the dignitaries, leaders, generals, admirals, and people with power and influence in his kingdom to prove to them why he deserved the title "King over all the earth."

After 180 days of extravagant feasting, Ahasuerus then threw open the doors and invited everyone else to the party.

And when these days were completed, the king gave a banquet lasting seven days for all the people who were present in Susa the capital, from the greatest to the least, in the court of the garden of the king's palace (Esther 1:5).

This meant that all the administrative staff, family, and friends were now invited. Some of the details of the palace are provided in this verse:

There were hangings of fine white and violet linen held by cords of fine purple linen on silver rings and marble columns, and couches of gold and silver on a mosaic of pavement . . . marble, mother-of-pearl, and precious stones (Esther 1:6).

The Persian word for garden is *paridaida*, which the Greeks pronounced *paradeisos*.[5] This is the same word borrowed by the English to give us the word *paradise*.

The banquet room was laden with fine linen, golden furniture, and gemstone mosaics. The great hall was so designed as to afford the hundreds of guests a view of the beautiful gardens as they dined.

Archeologists have discovered that the guests would have observed magnificent stone channels carrying water across acres of flowers and trees planted in symmetrical rows and creative patterns. The beauty of paradise was reflected in the water of lively ponds which framed the palace.

This place was a paradise . . . and the king of paradise was Ahasuerus.

To outsiders looking in, Ahasuerus seemed every bit the undefeatable, powerful sovereign who could—and would—subdue the kingdoms of earth and rule them.

Surely this king could command the greatest army the world had ever known.

But taking a closer look at his personal life—and with a touch of irony and humor—we discover that he cannot even command his own wife.

A LASCIVIOUS REQUEST

The reception of Ahasuerus was for men only, so Queen Vashti treated the women to their own banquet during the final seven-day period of the feast.

Queen Vashti also gave a banquet for the women in the palace which belonged to King Ahasuerus (Esther 1:9).

Historians believe this banquet included all 360 of the King's concubines.[6]

It's interesting to note that the name Vashti literally means desirable. It may very well have been an honorary title for her, since she was one of the king's favored wives.[7] Jewish tradition holds that Vashti was also the great-granddaughter of Nebuchadnezzar, the former king of Babylon.[8]

The queen was in the middle of enjoying her own dinner party when, all of a sudden, she was put in a precarious position. When the king was drunk with wine, he gave seven eunuchs the order to:

> **[B]ring Queen Vashti before the king with her royal crown in order to display her beauty to the people and the princes, for she was beautiful** (Esther 1:10-11).

In other words, King Ahasuerus had shown his splendor, his wealth, and his power for six months, but he decided that wasn't good enough. He still had one more prized possession to show off . . . his wife.

We know from history that Persian women did not cover their faces with veils. As the queen of the kingdom, Vashti had already appeared in public—more than likely, during this reception, as well as other state functions. Everyone already knew and could recognize the beautiful face of the king's most favored wife.

So what's really going on here?

The Jewish *Midrash*, a commentary dating all the way back to the second century, explained that the queen was being commanded to actually arrive *unclothed* . . . decorated only with her crown jewels.[9]

This is an embarrassing topic, but there's simply no way to sanitize it.

Esther 1:10 makes it clear that the king requested this **when his heart was merry with wine.** That's a nice way of saying the king was drunk. And you can be fairly confident that most, if not all, of his guests were drunk along with him.

So after 180 days of feasting and drinking, Ahasuerus desired to end his banquet not with fireworks, but with lust and envy: he wanted his guests to *envy* him and regard him as the only man who had the world by the tail.

Herodotus, the Greek historian who lived just after the Persian kingdom ended, wrote that this was common practice for Persian kings because the Persian people were so promiscuous. They loved parading their wives and concubines unclothed to show them off to one another. It was a competition—a little game of Let's See Who Has the Prettiest Wife.[10]

Frankly, this isn't surprising at all. Ahasuerus was the king. And he was a pagan with 360 concubines and several wives. You would expect this kind of debauchery from a godless man in a godless society. And while you might say, "How wicked is that?" the truth is we're not that far from Persia ourselves.

Persia is Daytona Beach during spring break. It's Mardi Gras in New Orleans. It's the Strip and "What happens in Vegas, stays in Vegas." It's the local "gentlemen's club"—where gentlemen are never found. It's the billion-dollar pornography business that grows more lucrative every year. It's the bachelor party you should have walked away from.

These are the all too common scenarios where women are paraded about, then tossed aside instead of being respected and loved by respectable, loving men.

The spirit of Ahasuerus is alive and well in our world today.

What Ahasuerus demanded was something other pagans might have expected from him. What we do *not* expect is the queen's response:

But Queen Vashti refused to come at the king's command delivered by the eunuchs (Esther 1:12*a*).

The drama screeches to a halt . . . the main character has refused to appear on stage.

The guests were shocked. Ahasuerus, the supreme commander who had been suggesting over the past six months that he could command the empires of the whole world, was being upstaged and embarrassed by a disobedient wife.

No wonder the king **became very angry and his wrath burned within him** (Esther 1:12*b*).

Imagine you're sitting in the audience watching this scene develop. The eunuchs have marched off stage to fetch the queen. There's a commotion backstage and you hear loud whispering. Something's very wrong—someone is obviously missing her cue. Suddenly the eunuchs appear onstage . . . without her.

The tension in the air is thick. No one breathes. Hands with food destined for mouths stop midair.

Can you imagine the poor eunuch going over to the king, leaning down and whispering in his ear, "Um, she said she's not gonna do it."

The king's face turns red, then purple. He has been denied—he has been disobeyed—and in front of hundreds of powerful guests he has been attempting to impress with his authority and majesty.

I love this scene.

The queen in the other room has just said, "Sorry, honey . . . it ain't happening," or however you say that in Persian.

The king was livid. "But I'm the king of the world . . . the ruler of nations . . . you can't say no to me!"

But she did.

Alexander Whyte, the nineteenth-century Scottish pastor who wrote wonderful character studies of both Old and New Testament figures, said this of Queen Vashti:

> The sacred writer makes us respect the queen amid all her disgusting surroundings. The brave queen refused to obey the royal order. Her beauty was her own and her husband's. It was not for open show among hundreds of half-drunk men.[11]

Well said.

I can't help but admire Vashti here. At that moment she displayed unusual character. She stood up to a man who had a known history for brutality.

But beyond that, she risked everything. Evidently, she was willing to sacrifice all the pomp and glamour and wealth. She'd rather walk away from *paradise* than become a sexual pawn . . . be shown off like chattel . . . be leered at by a banquet hall full of intoxicated men.

While Esther will soon replace her on the throne, don't miss the subtle irony in this contrast: Vashti sacrificed her crown to keep her character; Esther will sacrifice her character in order to win the crown.

Vashti deserves a minute of silent respect here. She's the queen we've never really thought about as we've rushed to meet her successor.

Early on in this drama, we're already confronted with the cost of character. How much is ours worth? How far are we willing to go in order to win praise or get attention? What will we sacrifice to get along with our peers?

Have you ever lost something because you did the right thing? Think sales contract, relationship, passing grade, job, sports game, etc.

Take heart from this dramatic presentation played out on the stage of history. Vashti knew it could cost her everything . . . but she also knew it was worth it.

Vashti's refusal also placed the king in a public predicament. He was supposedly able to command the greatest empire on the planet but had just been defied by his wife—and in front of all the dignitaries he was trying to convince to follow him into battle.

Now what he *should* have done was order a big pot of black coffee, sober up, and then apologize to his wife. Instead he sought advice from men who were paid to agree with him.

And the curtain falls on Scene II.

A LUDICROUS REACTION

Seven new actors now appear onstage. *Esther 1:13* tells us that they were wise men who knew the law and understood the times. They were the seven princes of the kingdom who **had access to the king's presence and sat in the first place in the kingdom** (Esther 1:14*b*).

In other words, this was his cabinet. They were his closest confidants.

He had just been royally embarrassed—literally—so he tried to save face and act like it was a matter of the law. He dismissed himself from the banquet and retreated with his seven counselors to figure out the best course of damage control. What the counselors eventually came up with is both foolish and funny at the same time.

The first thing they did was bandage the king's wounded ego (notice the exaggeration in their words):

> **And in the presence of the king and the other princes, Memucan said, "Queen Vashti has wronged not only the king but also all the princes, and all the peoples, who are in all the provinces of King Ahasuerus"** (Esther 1:16).

In other words, "This is a worldwide issue here, O great and slighted king—this will become a global crisis."

> **"For the queen's conduct will become known to all the women causing them to look with contempt on their husbands by saying, 'King Ahasuerus commanded Queen Vashti to be brought in to his presence, but she did not come.' And this day the ladies of Persia and Media who have heard of the queen's conduct will speak in the same way to all the king's princes, and there will be plenty of contempt and anger"** (Esther 1:17-18).

In other words, "We're all in trouble. If our wives hear about this, there will be a strike throughout the land. Skillets will fly through the air, laundry will pile up, meals will disappear . . . it will be total anarchy. We've got to stop this national disaster before it happens!"

They didn't even want to go home now.

So what was their brilliant solution to the problem?

"If it pleases the king, let a royal edict be issued by him and let it be written in the laws of Persia and Media so that it cannot be repealed, that Vashti should come no more into the presence of King Ahasuerus, and let the king give her royal position to another who is more worthy than she. And when the king's edict which he shall make is heard throughout all his kingdom, great as it is, then all women will give honor to their husbands, great and small" (Esther 1:19-20).

Now I know you guys are thinking, *That's a great idea. I like this book.*

If the edict wasn't specific enough, notice what the king adds to it: *"[E]very man should be the master in his own house"* (Esther 1:22*b*).

I think I could get used to this Law of the Medes and Persians. Can I get a copy of that edict?

I can just see some guy getting this royal edict in the mail and saying, "Oh, man . . . this is *exactly* what I've been waiting for." He tapes a copy above the kitchen sink . . . and in the living room above the television . . . and on the dash of the minivan. The moment his wife starts to talk back, all he has to do is point to the edict and say, "Don't forget what the king said."

Do any of you guys think this would work? Well, if you've been married longer than a few weeks, you've already learned that you can't legislate respect—you have to earn it. Respect is a gift you're given by your mate whom *you* respect. You aren't treated with honor by your wife or husband because you've got orders taped up around the house. You can't force respect and honor. These are sown and watered and fertilized before they bear fruit.

The king wanted respect from a woman he hadn't respected. He wanted honor from a wife he dishonored.

He said, "I'll just skip all that and make the respect of a wife for her husband a *law* of the Medes and Persians. Never mind sowing and watering and fertilizing—I want it *now.*"

The king's edict would only backfire. The stupidity of the wise men was amazing. First, they wanted to keep this embarrassing situation a secret but, by sending out a royal decree, they literally informed the entire nation of the incident.

Additionally, the king and his nobles were afraid that if the women found out about Vashti's defiance, they would stop obeying their husbands. Yet Ahasuerus sent the edict to every household, ensuring that every woman *would* hear of Vashti's disobedience.

Who came up with this idea?

No wonder the Jews throughout the ages have howled with laughter at the foolishness of the king and his "wise" men . . . who obviously must have still been drunk.

Actually, those men had all sobered up by now.

While they may have seemed to be acting under the influence of the king's wine, they were really acting according to the influence of *the* King of king's *will*.

No matter how untimely or difficult the events of our life become, don't miss this truth parading across a Persian stage: God is backstage directing it all.

His hand is not just resting in the glove of history, it's resting in the glove of *our* history—past, present, and future.

No matter how helpless we might feel as our own drama unfolds, God is managing every scene to fulfill His purposes in our life.

He may be hidden in the shadows backstage; He may not have published a playbill that explains every scene in our life, outlining every important character and event, but **He's running the show**.

One author wrote:

Don't fall into the trap of thinking that God is asleep when it comes to nations or that He is out of touch when it comes to carnal banquets or that He sits in heaven wringing His hands when it comes to godless rulers who make unfair, rash, or even foolish decisions. This is the wonder of God's providence—working behind the scenes, bringing out of even the most carnal and secular of settings a decision that will set His perfect plan in place.[12]

So as the curtain closes on the final scene of Act 1 in this divine drama, don't miss the way God is working behind the scenes to bring everything together. He is using a banished queen, an angry king, and a vacant throne to set the stage for the rest of the play. The introductory act is complete . . . the *real* drama is about to begin.

After these things when the anger of King Ahasuerus had subsided, he remem-
bered Vashti and what she had done and what had been decreed against her.
²Then the king's attendants, who served him, said, "Let beautiful young virgins
be sought for the king. ³And let the king appoint overseers in all the provinces
of his kingdom that they may gather every beautiful young virgin to Susa the
capital, to the harem, into the custody of Hegai, the king's eunuch, who was in
charge of the women; and let their cosmetics be given them. ⁴Then let the young
lady who pleases the king be queen in place of Vashti." And the matter pleased
the king, and he did accordingly. ⁵Now there was a Jew in Susa the capital
whose name was Mordecai, the son of Jair, the son of Shimei, the son of Kish, a
Benjamite, ⁶who had been taken into exile from Jerusalem with the captives who
had been exiled with Jeconiah king of Judah, whom Nebuchadnezzar the king
of Babylon had exiled. ⁷And he was bringing up Hadassah, that is Esther, his
uncle's daughter, for she had neither father nor mother. Now the young lady was
beautiful of form and face, and when her father and her mother died, Mordecai

(Continued on next page)

(Continued)

took her as his own daughter. ⁸*So it came about when the command and decree of the king were heard and many young ladies were gathered to Susa the capital into the custody of Hegai, that Esther was taken to the king's palace into the custody of Hegai, who was in charge of the women.* ⁹*Now the young lady pleased him and found favor with him. So he quickly provided her with her cosmetics and food, gave her seven choice maids from the king's palace, and transferred her and her maids to the best place in the harem.* ¹⁰*Esther did not make known her people or her kindred, for Mordecai had instructed her that she should not make them known.* ¹¹*And every day Mordecai walked back and forth in front of the court of the harem to learn how Esther was and how she fared.* ¹²*Now when the turn of each young lady came to go in to King Ahasuerus, after the end of her twelve months under the regulations for the women—for the days of their beautification were completed as follows: six months with oil of myrrh and six months with spices and the cosmetics for women—*¹³*the young lady would go in to the king in this way: anything that she desired was given her to take with her from the harem to the king's palace.* ¹⁴*In the evening she would go in and in the morning she would return to the second harem, to the custody of Shaashgaz, the king's eunuch who was in charge of the concubines. She would not again go in to the king unless the king delighted in her and she was summoned by name.* ¹⁵*Now when the turn of Esther, the daughter of Abihail the uncle of Mordecai who had taken her as his daughter, came to go in to the king, she did not request anything except what Hegai, the king's eunuch who was in charge of the women, advised. And Esther found favor in the eyes of all who saw her.* ¹⁶*So Esther was taken to King Ahasuerus to his royal palace in the tenth month which is the month Tebeth, in the seventh year of his reign.* ¹⁷*And the king loved Esther more than all the women, and she found favor and kindness with him more than all the virgins, so that he set the royal crown on her head and made her queen instead of Vashti.* ¹⁸*Then the king gave a great banquet, Esther's banquet, for all his princes and his servants; he also made a holiday for the provinces and gave gifts according to the king's bounty.* ¹⁹*And when the virgins were gathered together the second time, then Mordecai was sitting at the king's gate.* ²⁰*Esther had not yet made known her kindred or her people, even as Mordecai had commanded her, for Esther did what Mordecai told her as she had done when under his care.*

–Esther 2:1-20

CHAPTER THREE

THE CONTEST AND THE CROWN

Esther 2:1-20

THE LOVING SOVEREIGN LINGERS

A Christian magazine recently featured a number of humorous things on the subject of love and romance.

My favorite told of a single woman who was tired of looking for Mr. Right. She had tried for so long to find a nice guy who would shower her with attention and act like a gentleman, but nothing had worked. She finally placed an ad in the classifieds that simply read, "Husband wanted."

The next day she got a dozen calls from women, all saying the same thing: "You can have mine!"

This article also reported some of the funny things kids said about the subject.

When asked how love *happens*, a third-grader named Hannah said, "No one's sure how it happens, but I think it has something to do with how you smell."

I think she's been talking to my dog.

When asked what it means to fall in love, nine-year-old Nate said, "Falling in love is like an avalanche—and you better run for your life!"

Asked how to make a marriage work, Ian said, "You need to tell your wife she looks pretty even when she looks like a truck."

Evidently he's been married before.

Another boy added, "You gotta find somebody who likes the same stuff. If you like sports, she should like 'em, too; and she should keep the chips and dip coming."

Now there's a marriage made in heaven.

How do you decide which person you should actually marry? According to one little girl, "Well . . . you see . . . no person *really* decides before they grow up who they're going to marry. *God* decides it way before and you get to find out later who you're *stuck* with."

Makes you wonder if her mother married that chip-and-dip guy.

I find it fascinating that in almost every romantic story—whether in movies, books, or real life—some things are almost universally accepted as romantic. Flowers, cards, candy, chivalry, kindness, and . . . yes, even a little perfume are just a few.

Romance is what fairytales are made of.

And that's why the Book of Esther has all the trappings of a good fairytale: there's a beautiful maiden, a lonely king, a kingdom-wide pageant, and a stunning palace. At first glance, it might strike you as some kind of real-life Cinderella story.

But as we go further into our study of Esther, we'll discover that it isn't a love story at all—or at least, not between a prince and princess.

The only love in this story is that of a faithful God for His prodigal people.

When the curtain closed at the end of the first chapter of Esther, we had to wait several years before the story picked up again. In the interim, Ahasuerus had marshaled the largest Persian army in history and tried to accomplish what his father never could: crush and dominate Greece. One inscription actually revealed that he intended to conquer all of Europe, as well.

Western civilization wouldn't be what it is today, had this former king of Persia been victorious. Instead, the Greeks routed his army and demolished most of his navy. Ahasuerus eventually boarded a ship and sailed home, sullen and dispirited.[1]

THE LOSING KING RETURNS

The curtain rises on Act II with the spotlight on the defeated king:

After these things [that is, after the Persian war with Greece] *when the anger of King Ahasuerus had subsided, he remembered Vashti*

and what she had done and what had been decreed against her.
Then the king's attendants, who served him, said, "Let beautiful
young virgins be sought for the king . . . Then let the young lady
who pleases the king be queen in place of Vashti" (Esther 2:1-2, 4*a*).

We know historically that kings had many concubines; they were considered "lesser wives." They also had numerous wives of higher rank who could wear the crown at any time depending on the whim of the king.

History bears out that one of Ahasuerus' higher-ranking wives Amenstris had borne him a son whom he chose as heir to the throne.[2] Amenstris had either passed away or no longer had the king's favor during this time. We don't know why, but the Bible informs us that Vashti had taken her place for a brief season as the favored wife.

But now with Vashti gone, there was a void in the royal palace, as well as the king's heart—he regretted his decision to banish her.

The Hebrew construction of *Esther 2:1* strongly implies that Ahasuerus blamed his seven counselors for persuading him to banish the queen.

He wasn't in a good mood.

His troops had been depleted, as had his war chest; his credibility throughout the empire was sorely bruised; his "king of kings" title had been lost and, now, when he returned home, he faced the daunting reminder that his favorite wife was gone.

Little wonder that his seven counselors approached him with an intriguing proposition: "Listen, O great king—why don't we have an empire-wide beauty contest and find you another queen. What do you say?"

This might not seem like an odd request to us, but to the Persians it would have been unheard of. According to Herodotus, the Persian custom required that the queen be related to one of the seven noble families.[3] So what in the world were those counselors thinking?

Some scholars believe that Memucan (the leading noble who initially verbalized the idea of getting rid of Vashti) had a marriageable relative in his own family and hoped she would win the crown. Regardless, he and his six friends knew they were in deep trouble if they didn't come up with a solution . . . and fast.

The king needed a beautiful replacement for Vashti, and they didn't dare recommend one of their own relatives. This was the reason those seven nobles actually went *against* Persian tradition—something they normally defended—to suggest that the queen be chosen from the *common* people of the empire.

This kind of thing had never been done in Persian history.

We have a real Cinderella story in the making . . . and only a God as great as ours could use all the political intrigue to pull off what He had in mind.

The counselors' plan is spelled out for us:

> **"[L]***et the king appoint overseers in all the provinces of his king-***
> ***dom*** [remember . . . this kingdom stretches from Africa to India]
> ***that they may gather every beautiful young virgin to Susa the***
> ***capital, to the harem, into the custody of Hegai, the king's eunuch,***
> ***who is in charge of the women; and let their cosmetics be given***
> ***them. Then let the young lady who pleases the king be queen in***
> ***place of Vashti." And the matter pleased the king, and he did***
> ***accordingly*** (Esther 2:3-4).

To the citizens of Persia, this was a once-in-a-lifetime opportunity. Any young woman could apply. Any unmarried peasant actually had a chance to become queen.

This was the talk in every town and village throughout Persia: "Who will win the crown?" The streets must have been filled with excitement and frenzy upon hearing this news, with thousands standing in line as they anxiously awaited the arrival of the king's attendants.

A woman only needed to be a virgin . . . and young . . . and beautiful.

Memberships at Weight Watchers went through the roof. Women were lying about their age in unprecedented numbers. And why not? The prize was the crown and the wealth and the footmen and the handmaids and the money and the food and the leisure and the clothing—the winner got it all.

Happily Ever After was waiting.

But before we get too caught up in what looks to be a normal, run-of-the-mill fairytale, don't forget what this contest is really about. There's no way to purify what will happen in the next scene of this story.

There will be only one judge . . . the performances will be private.

Make no mistake about this: behind the imperial mask of pomp and pageantry, there was the face of debauchery, selfishness, and lust. It was anything *but* love.

The palace eunuchs were given the administrative oversight of the harem. They kept close watch over the women because of the drama that took place every day created by the competition and feuding. Most of those women would never get past their one-night stand with the king.

The losers would transition to the king's harem to live forgotten lives, sequestered away in the palace at Susa. One commentator called the harem of the kings "luxurious desolation." [4]

THE LEADING CHARACTERS APPEAR

Now there was a Jew in Susa the capital whose name was Mordecai, the son of Jair, the son of Shimei, the son of Kish, a Benjamite, who had been taken into exile from Jerusalem with the captives who had been exiled with Jeconiah king of Judah, whom Nebuchadnezzar the king of Babylon had exiled (Esther 2:5-6).

As soon as we're introduced to Mordecai we discover that he came from a royal family. Mordecai's lineage dates back to King Saul.[5] In fact, he and his cousin were descendants of what used to be the royal tribe in Israel. But regardless of this, Mordecai's name doesn't bear any resemblance to his Jewish lineage. His name is simply the transliteration of Marduk, the chief Babylonian god.[6]

So what's a good Jewish man from the tribe of Benjamin doing in a place like Susa? And why didn't he return to Jerusalem when the Persian captivity ended? Furthermore, why is he named after a pagan god, for goodness sake?

The answer to all these questions might be found in Mordecai's family history.

Hundreds of years earlier, when King David was running for his life from Absalom, Mordecai's forefather Shimei threw rocks at David and cursed him for stealing away Saul's throne. David's son Solomon later put Shimei to death. If Mordecai knew all this, then perhaps Jerusalem represented a place of defeat for him. It was the place where his family had lost their bid for power—a place of embarrassment and shame.

It's no surprise, then, that he decided to settle in Persia, just as his father had willingly been absorbed into the Persian culture before him. The evidence of his own father's abandonment of his Jewish heritage is seen in the fact that he named his son after a pagan god.

At this point in the story Mordecai was so Persianized that his Jewish heritage was the best kept secret in the land. Nobody knew he was a Jew . . . and he intended to keep it that way.

Before we get all hot and bothered about Mordecai's secret, I can't help but wonder how much of a secret our own relationship with Jesus Christ is. In the kingdom that surrounds us every day—the office or classroom or gym or neighborhood—are we keeping Jesus Christ to ourselves?

Does anyone know we're a Christian?

I can't tell you how many people have said to me over my years of pastoring something like, "I'm not very good at talking about Christ, so I just live it." There's an ancient Hebrew word for that attitude and it's pronounced *cop out*!

Has it ever occurred to you that no one will ever be saved by watching you? Certainly we need to make sure that what we *say* and what they *see* matches up.

But if people don't know *why* we're living the way we are, they'll most likely give *us* the credit. The only way they can see our good works that glorify our Father in heaven is if we give glory to Him. We need to tell them *He's* the reason we're living the way we are and doing the things we do.

Paul says that **faith comes from hearing, and hearing by the word of Christ** (Romans 10:17). Salvation doesn't come by watching—it comes by hearing.

It takes a messenger who is willing to deliver special revelation to someone in order for them to be saved. So let's not keep our Christianity a secret like Mordecai hid his Jewishness in the kingdom of Persia.

THE LUXURIOUS CONTEST BEGINS

For the first time in the Book of Esther, we are finally introduced to the main character; Esther is about to grace the stage.

> **And he was bringing up Hadassah, that is Esther, his uncle's daughter, for she had no father or mother. Now the young lady was beautiful of form and face, and when her father and her mother died, Mordecai took her as his own daughter** (Esther 2:7).

This time we're given both the Hebrew name Hadassah, which refers to the flower of a myrtle bush, and her pagan name Esther, which is most likely a transliteration of Ishtar, the Babylonian goddess of love.[7]

Evidently Esther was left orphaned at childhood by the death of her parents, and Mordecai, who was 15 years older than she, adopted her as his own child. When Mordecai got wind of the contest, he immediately saw their chance to climb the ladder of success.

He saw the procession in the street. He heard the gossip on the lips of every villager. He knew Esther was incredibly beautiful, and he most likely had been driving away suitors for the past few years.

Now he finally had a chance to cash in on his cousin's good looks. He could use her beauty as a means to further his ambition for his own career.

So it came about when the command and decree of the king were heard and many young ladies were gathered to Susa the capital into the custody of Hegai, that Esther was taken to the king's palace into the custody of Hegai, who was in charge of the women (Esther 2:8).

I can think of at least three good reasons why Esther shouldn't stand a chance at winning the contest.

1. **She was an orphan.** She had no family connections. She offered the king no beneficial arrangement between families of wealth or nobility. Esther was an ordinary peasant girl—a nobody.

2. **She was up against fierce competition.** According to Josephus, the first-century Jewish historian, this contest had attracted more than 1,000 young women. The palace was swarming with beautiful women. Esther wasn't the only girl turning heads.

3. **She was a Jewess.** Jews were the people of a defeated nation—outsiders who had adopted Persian ways but were still not truly Persian. And if the news leaked out that she was a Jew, whatever slim chance she might have had of winning would immediately go down the tubes. She might be chosen for the harem but never for the crown.

That's why we read that ***Esther did not make known her people or her kindred, for Mordecai had instructed her that she should not make them known*** (Esther 2:10).

Mordecai was effectively saying to Esther, "Israel is in the past. God might have made you a Jewess, but it won't do you any good here. Out here you have to live by your wits . . . you have to fend for yourself."

"Don't ever forget, Esther," Mordecai was implying, "out here, we're on our own . . . it's all up to us."

But he couldn't have been further from the truth. In fact, God was already at work directing this traffic jam of contestants.

The first thing God did was give her favor with everyone in the palace. Of Hegai, the chief administrator of this contest, it was said: ***Now the young lady pleased him and found favor with him*** (Esther 2:9*a*).

That word "favor" is the Hebrew word *khesed*, which is the same term used for God's covenant favor and kindness toward His people. We see it again here: ***And Esther found favor in the eyes of all who saw her*** (Esther 2:15*c*).

Frankly, this is shocking. You would expect to read, "Esther found envy in the eyes of all who saw her" . . . or anger . . . or jealousy. You would imagine that the other contestants were planning to bump her off and hide the body. This is a competition, after all. And all 1,000 contestants are in it to win it.

There was simply no explanation for this universal favor other than the fact that God was turning the hearts of everyone toward her.

Don't miss this: **God may be invisible, but He is still involved. His hand is invisible, but His plan is invincible.**

Esther was in Hegai's good favor:

So he quickly provided her with her cosmetics [Avon calling.] ***and food, gave her seven choice maids from the king's palace and transferred her and her maids to the best place in the harem*** (Esther 2:9*b*).

Within a matter of hours, Esther was given her own private suite, seven maids, and plenty to eat and drink. She did nothing but relax in the royal spa.

The same can't be said of poor Mordecai:

And every day Mordecai walked back and forth in front of the court of the harem to learn how Esther was and how she fared (Esther 2:11).

He was biting his nails . . . on pins and needles. He was probably think-ing to himself, *What have I done? She's in there with a thousand contestants. She's naïve—she'll never keep her secret—she doesn't stand a chance. There's gotta be something I can do to make this work in her favor.*

What he didn't know was that God was already working things out in her favor . . . and without any help from Mordecai.

He was about to learn that he wasn't sovereign over Esther's life—God was.

While he paced anxiously in front of the building, he had no clue that Esther was being pampered inside. She wasn't a queen yet, but she was being treated like one:

> *Now when the turn of each young lady came to go in to King Ahasuerus, after the end of her twelve months under the regula-tions for the women—for the days of their beautification were completed as follows: six months with oil of myrrh and six months with spices and the cosmetics for women* (Esther 2:12).

What a life. Twelve months?. And we think our wives and daughters take a long time to get ready to go out.

The oil of myrrh was used to soften and lighten the skin. Since most of the women had worked outdoors, their skin was darkened by the sun and calloused from their labors.

To the Persians, fair skin was a sign of beauty. It took around twelve months of massage therapy and indoor living to soften and lighten the com-plexion of the women.[8]

Historians tell us that the king's harem swam in perfumed water. The treatments of myrrh and make-up had become an intricate science of cos-metics. The Persians didn't just wear make-up for beauty's sake . . . they wore it for *spiritual* reasons.

The priests of Persia were the ones who developed and protected the formulas and practices of cosmetics. Because they saw the physical as merely a gateway to the spiritual, they truly believed that cleanliness was, indeed, next to godliness. Smell was believed to be connected with divine acceptance.

Women wore make-up around their eyes and bracelets around their arms, necks, and feet to ward off evil spirits. They were given rouge for their cheeks, all shades of lipstick, eyeliner, and fingernail polish because they believed that beauty brought them closer to the gods. And in a matter of months they would be led before a man most closely connected to the gods—the king himself.

Along with this beautification process, the thousand contestants were also being schooled in court customs and royal etiquette. As one scholar noted, they were learning what to say and how to say it.[9] They had come straight from the fields and many of them were unschooled, illiterate, and untrained. But they were beautiful. And at the end of one year, one of them would sit on the throne as queen.

So this year-long process was actually a crash course on how to look like a queen, sound like a queen, act like a queen, eat like a queen, and smell like a queen.

And at this point in the story Esther didn't seem to be protesting. Unlike Daniel before her, she wasn't refusing to eat the meat or drink the wine which had been offered to idols.[10]

In this drama, she was a character without godly character . . . and she kept her secret safely hidden away.

THE LOWLY COMMONER IS CROWNED

As much as theologians and pastors would like to pretty up this next scene, it's frankly impossible. One author said this contest would become nothing less than a sordid meat market.[11] Esther, along with a thousand other young women (no doubt many of them Jewish, as well), would lose her virginity to a pagan Gentile.

And only one would be chosen to wear the crown.

Jewish rabbis attempted to clean this up by adding verses to the original text found in the Septuagint (the Greek translation of the Hebrew text).

Some of the rabbinical additions tried to reconcile Esther's character by having her claim she never violated the dietary kosher laws of the Hebrews. In one verse they actually have her pray these words to God: "You know everything; and you know that I hate the pomp of the wicked, and the bed of the uncircumcised and any foreigner."[12]

These are obvious attempts to sanctify the actions of Esther and keep her in heroic form.

Some evangelical authors have taken a different approach at exonerating Esther from blame. They make the case that Esther *was taken to King Ahasuerus* (Esther 2:16*a*), and the verb "taken" implied it was against her will.

The problem with this interpretation is that the same verb is found in the previous verse, where we're told that *Mordecai took her as his daughter* (Esther 2:15*a*).

This interpretation just doesn't line up. As unfortunate as it sounds, Esther wasn't taken by force—she went willingly.

She didn't put the brakes on, but she did have her best outfit on. Her face was prepared with make-up, her body drenched in perfume, and her mind made up: she would practice the secrets given to her by the chief eunuch who wanted to see her win the crown.

> *So Esther was taken to King Ahasuerus to his royal palace in the tenth month, which is the month Tebeth, in the seventh year of his reign. And the king loved Esther more than all the women, and she found favor and kindness with him more than all the virgins, so that he set the royal crown on her head and made her queen instead of Vashti* (Esther 2:16-17).

Esther won the contest. She was now Miss Persia. But all the cheers and applause sound hollow, don't they? Was winning the crown worth her virginity? . . . her integrity?

I can't help but wonder how many young women have sacrificed themselves to keep that boyfriend who said, "If you love me, you will."

I wonder how many professionals have kept their faith a secret so it didn't get in the way of their climb up the corporate ladder.

I wonder how many Christians are living like Persians because they just want to get along with the Persians.

So . . . let me tell you what Esther *lost*.

Esther might have gained the title of Queen, but she didn't gain a husband. *The king loved Esther more than all the women* (Esther 2:17*a*), but he still loved the other women, too.

The text never says, "And after the crowning of Esther, the king ordered that his harem be released and his concubines, also."

Not even close:

***And when the virgins were gathered together the second time, then
Mordecai was sitting at the gate*** (Esther 2:19).

Why was there a *second* time? Esther had already won the crown—somebody stop the contest.

They did.

This second gathering of virgins had nothing to do with a contest. It had
everything to do with the king's ever-expanding harem.

Esther would occupy the throne as queen, but she would not be the sole
occupant of the king's bed. In fact, her role wouldn't even allow her unhin-
dered access to his bedroom . . . or his life.

Furthermore, Esther won the crown, but she didn't win an honest relationship. She had a secret. In fact, it would be five years before she told her
husband who she really was—and then it was almost too late.

But as bad as all this sounds, it would have been a lot worse for her had
she lost the contest. Look what happened to the losers:

> **[T]***he young lady would go in to the king in this way: anything
> that she desired was given her to take with her from the harem
> to the king's palace. In the evening she would go in and in the
> morning she would return to the second harem, to the custody
> of Shaashgaz, the king's eunuch who was in charge of the con-
> cubines. She would not again go in to the king unless the king
> delighted in her and she was summoned by name*** (Esther 2:13-14).

Did you catch that? Women went in as young ladies and came out as
concubines, relegated thereafter to a life of *luxurious desolation*. They would
never be called on again unless the king happened to remember their names.
The king, however, wasn't in the habit of remembering names—he was in
the habit of *adding* names.

So God, in His grace, put Esther at the front of the line. Out of all the
hundreds of women who came and went in the contest, she would be the
one the king would crown.

This reveals to us an amazing truth about the character of God: He works
through faithful people and in spite of unfaithful people. The providence
of God is the way in which God leads through people who will not be led.

His providence is unstoppable. How grateful we are that He lavishes His grace on us even when we don't deserve it. I suppose that's why we call it *grace*.

Have you ever thought about the grace of God, even when you sin against Him? Mind-boggling truth that it is, God is faithful to extend grace even when we are unfaithful.

This doesn't mean we can sin all we want just so grace can be demonstrated even more. When the Apostle Paul wrote **where sin increased, grace abounded all the more** (Romans 5:20*b*), he wasn't giving us license to sin. Many thought he was, at the time.

Paul was simply revealing just how measureless the grace of God is toward His children. The amazing truth is that even when we disobey God—which is daily—He never leaves us nor forsakes us.

That's what we find throughout Esther's story. She was drenched in more than just myrrh and Persian perfume. She was drenched in the grace of God. The aroma of His kindness toward her permeated the pages of her story from cover to cover.

This was the grace of God, in spite of Esther's violations of the law—in spite of the fact that she kept her heritage a secret. Here's the evidence of the grace of God: He turned the heart of that vile king so that he chose Esther to be his queen. He didn't really know all the reasons why. But God did.

God was the One who placed Esther on the throne . . . not Ahasuerus. And God didn't choose Esther because she was more beautiful than the others or because she was more worthy than another. God chose her because He planned to use her to bring about the deliverance of His people.

God was the One who gave Esther her beauty to begin with. God was the One who gave her a rich Jewish heritage. God was the One who placed her in Persia at such an opportune time.

Why? Because He had made a promise to Israel's forefathers that He would make of them an everlasting people. Because He had promised that from the Jewish people, the Savior of the world would come . . . the Messiah.

So *nothing*—not even this little so-called "king of the world"—could stand in the way of God's plan. And the curtain rings down on Act II.

What will Esther learn, along with the rest of us? When God makes a promise, He keeps it.

Do you want to live a satisfied life? Trust God.

Do you want to see God at work? Join him and co-labor with Him in His global search for worshippers.

Do you want to make a difference in your world? Stop focusing on the reflection in the mirror and let your world know you belong to Him.

In the meantime, remember: you shouldn't *test* providence . . . you *trust* it.

²¹ *In those days, while Mordecai was sitting at the king's gate, Bigthan and Teresh, two of the king's officials from those who guarded the door, became angry and sought to lay hands on King Ahasuerus.* ²² *But the plot became known to Mordecai, and he told Queen Esther, and Esther informed the king in Mordecai's name.* ²³ *Now when the plot was investigated and found to be so, they were both hanged on a gallows; and it was written in the Book of the Chronicles in the king's presence.*

—Esther 2:21-23

After these events King Ahasuerus promoted Haman, the son of Hammedatha the Agagite, and advanced him and established his authority over all the princes who were with him. ² *And all the king's servants who were at the king's gate bowed down and paid homage to Haman; for so the king had commanded concerning*

(Continued on next page)

him. But Mordecai neither bowed down nor paid homage. ³Then the king's servants who were at the king's gate said to Mordecai, "Why are you transgressing the king's command?" ⁴Now it was when they had spoken daily to him and he would not listen to them, that they told Haman to see whether Mordecai's reason would stand; for he had told them that he was a Jew. ⁵When Haman saw that Mordecai neither bowed down nor paid homage to him, Haman was filled with rage. ⁶But he disdained to lay hands on Mordecai alone, for they had told him who the people of Mordecai were; therefore Haman sought to destroy all the Jews, the people of Mordecai, who were throughout the whole kingdom of Ahasuerus. ⁷In the first month, which is the month Nisan, in the twelfth year of King Ahasuerus, Pur, that is the lot, was cast before Haman from day to day and from month to month, until the twelfth month, that is the month of Adar. ⁸Then Haman said to King Ahasuerus, "There is a certain people scattered and dispersed among the peoples in all the provinces of your kingdom; their laws are different from those of all other people, and they do not observe the king's laws, so it is not in the king's interest to let them remain. ⁹If it is pleasing to the king, let it be decreed that they be destroyed, and I will pay ten thousand talents of silver into the hands of those who carry on the king's business, to put into the king's treasuries." ¹⁰Then the king took his signet ring from his hand and gave it to Haman, the son of Hammedatha the Agagite, the enemy of the Jews. ¹¹And the king said to Haman, "The silver is yours, and the people also, to do with them as you please." ¹²Then the king's scribes were summoned on the thirteenth day of the first month, and it was written just as Haman commanded to the king's satraps, to the governors who were over each province, and to the princes of each people, each province according to its script, each people according to its language, being written in the name of King Ahasuerus and sealed with the king's signet ring. ¹³And letters were sent by couriers to all the king's provinces to destroy, to kill, and to annihilate all the Jews, both young and old, women and children, in one day, the thirteenth day of the twelfth month, which is the month Adar, and to seize their possessions as plunder. ¹⁴A copy of the edict to be issued as law in every province was published to all the peoples so that they should be ready for this day. ¹⁵The couriers went out impelled by the king's command while the decree was issued in Susa the capital; and while the king and Haman sat down to drink, the city of Susa was in confusion.

–Esther 3:1-15

CHAPTER FOUR

FAMILY FEUD

Esther 2:21-3:15

MANKIND'S DEVILISH PERPETRATOR

Without a doubt, the most famous family feud in American history was between the Hatfield and McCoy families.

The Hatfields and the McCoys lived on either side of a creek named Tug Fork. That creek served as the geographical border between Kentucky and West Virginia—the McCoys settling on the Kentucky side and the Hatfields living on the West Virginia side.

In 1878, McCoy accused Hatfield's family of slipping across Tug Fork and stealing one of his hogs. Hog-stealing was a very serious offense back in those days, and Mr. McCoy took Mr. Hatfield to court over it. Unfortunately, he didn't have enough evidence to bring about a conviction and the jury found the Hatfields innocent.

After the trial was over, someone from the McCoy family was so angry that he shot and killed a juror who had sided with the Hatfields.

Everything went downhill after that.

Four years after the shooting, one of the McCoys ran for public office. He was verbally attacked and discredited publicly by one of the Hatfields and lost the race as a result. A blood bath erupted, and after the final shot, three McCoys were dead, including the politically ambitious son.

But the fighting didn't end there; those who supported either family along the border of Kentucky and West Virginia joined in the fray.

The feud reached its peak in the 1888 New Year's Night Massacre, or so it was called, when several of the Hatfields surrounded the McCoy homestead and opened fire on the sleeping family. They also set the house on fire in an effort to drive Randolph McCoy out into the open. He managed to slip away and escaped the fire, but his family wasn't so fortunate. His two children were killed that night, and his wife was left for dead.

The Hatfields and McCoys were often headline news throughout the country and at one point the governors of Kentucky and West Virginia called up their state militias to try to restore order.

When all was said and done, this family feud cost the lives of dozens of people—from both sides of Tug Fork.

And it all began with a stolen pig.

In *Esther 2*, we witness a family fracas that could prove far more devastating than the Hatfield/McCoy feud. Instead of taking the lives of dozens of people, it could kill tens of thousands.

It was the feud between Mordecai's family and Haman's family.

Many Old Testament scholars believe it was no coincidence that both Haman's and Mordecai's family tree are explicitly given in this book. Haman's ancestry reveals why his reason to massacre the Jewish people wasn't just a political decision . . . it was personal.

The bad blood dated all the way back to *Exodus 17*, where the Amalekites became the very first nation in the world to attack God's newly formed covenant nation.[1] Though the Amalekites were defeated in that battle, they spent the next 900 years growing more bitter against the God of Israel . . . and His people.

In the First Book of Samuel, King Saul was ordered to bring the judgment of God against the Amalekites and their king Agag. Instead of obeying God, however, Saul spared Agag and the best of the cattle. The prophet Samuel indicted Saul for his disobedience and then executed Agag himself (*1 Samuel 15:33*).

With Agag dead, his descendants scattered, taking their hatred for God *and* the Jews with them wherever they settled.

While clashes between the two nations often erupted in bloodshed, the Book of Esther provides the dramatic climax of their family feud. In fact, the threat against the Jews was never more dangerous:

> ***Then the king took his signet ring from his hand and gave it to Haman, the son of Hammedatha, the Agagite, the enemy of the Jews*** (Esther 3:10).

As Ezra wrote this account, he didn't want us to miss the real issue here. This wasn't about a stolen pig. This feud represented the hatred of the world for the people of God.

And did you notice how Scripture describes Haman? It says he was *the enemy of the Jews*. Why? Haman was a descendant of King Agag. He was going to attempt to settle the score—to kill all the Jews throughout the Persian Empire and succeed where his ancestors had failed.

What Ezra wanted us to understand as he penned this God-inspired account was that this feud wasn't just between Mordecai and Haman.

On the surface, we could trace it back to a defeated nation, an executed king, a deposed family, and wounded pride to discover Haman's reasons for hating the Jews.

But beneath it all, we'll discover that the reason for his vengeance had nothing to do with his family tree. Haman's hatred was actually inspired by the Jews' real enemy—Satan himself—who had been trying for centuries to destroy God's covenant nation in order to ensure that God couldn't fulfill His promises.

This was more than an ongoing feud between the Amalakites and the Israelites . . . it was an age-old conflict between the Kingdom of Darkness and the Kingdom of Light.

Haman, like Agag before him, was just a pawn in the hand of a desperate devil who would spend all of history trying to destroy God's beloved people. King Agag wasn't the first to attack the Jews and—as we know full well—his descendant Haman wouldn't be the last.

With that as a backdrop, Act III of our drama opens, and *Mordecai was sitting at the king's gate* (Esther 2:21).

MORDECAI'S DESIRED PROMOTION

We notice right away that Mordecai had been promoted in the palace—no doubt, due to Esther's influence. When we read *Mordecai was sitting at the gate*, we might be tempted to think that he was sitting at the end of the king's driveway, checking license plates as people drove up to the palace . . . which doesn't sound like much of a promotion to me.

But the King's Gate was actually the administration building just inside the palace complex, where legal, civil, and commercial business was transacted on the king's behalf.[2]

When archeologists excavated the palace at Susa, they discovered that the King's Gate was actually 12,000 square feet in size. An inscription by Ahasuerus was found, which revealed that the gate had been built earlier by his father Darius.

So to be inside the King's Gate meant a person was one of the power brokers of the kingdom. He was in the inner circle. He went to office parties at the palace and received a gift from the king on his birthday—probably a towel or mug monogrammed with Ahasuerus' insignia.

Mordecai had officially arrived. He'd moved into the West Wing, next to the Oval Office.

But while he was working diligently on the king's business, some of his staff members informed him of a plot to kill the king.

THE EUNUCHS' DEADLY PLOT

In those days, while Mordecai was sitting at the king's gate, Bigthan and Teresh, two of the king's officials from those who guarded the door, became angry and sought to lay hands on King Ahasaurus (Esther 2:21).

Those men didn't want to shake hands with the king . . . they wanted to *lay hands* on him.

So who, exactly, were they? The verse tells us they **guarded the door**, which means they stood just outside the Oval Office. They were the last line of defense for the king.[3]

We're not told why they wanted to kill him, but the fact that they were eunuchs provides the perfect motive.

Herodotus reports that as many as 500 young boys were gathered from subjugated nations each year and castrated to serve as eunuchs.[4] It was a brutal policy that revealed how everyone—from beautiful virgins to young boys—was at the disposal of the king's personal desires.

Eunuchs were typically entrusted with caring for the king's harem, but many of them became leading officials throughout the ancient empires.

One of the most famous eunuchs in Scripture was the prophet Daniel, who was taken by Nebuchadnezzar, king of Babylon, when Jerusalem was destroyed. Instead of growing bitter because of his abduction and inability to later marry and father children, he became a faithful, hardworking ambassador for his true and living God. He eventually led political rulers to faith in Israel's God.

But Daniel was a rare case. Often in ancient history, eunuchs were involved in palace uprisings. So it's not really surprising to learn in *Esther 2* that those eunuchs were planning to assassinate the king.

Their attempt failed, however. Josephus tells us that a eunuch's servant overheard the plot and told Mordecai.[5] We pick up the story where the historian relates that *he* [Mordecai] *told Queen Esther, and Esther informed the king in Mordecai's name* (Esther 2:22).

> *Now when the plot was investigated and found to be so, they were both hanged on a gallows; and it was written in the Book of the Chronicles in the king's presence* (Esther 2:23).

Esther had made sure she mentioned the name of the king's most loyal administrator. Now Mordecai was a hero—he saved the king's life. You'd think Ahasuerus would've given him a gold watch or a pay raise or a week-long vacation. But what did the king do?

Nothing.

For some odd reason, he completely overlooked Mordecai; no pay increase for Mordecai. No pat on the back for his loyalty. No "thanks for saving my skin" or "take three extra days off."

This was strange because, according to history, acts of loyalty were usually rewarded immediately and generously by Persian kings. So there wasn't any *logical* or *historical* explanation why Mordecai's reward was overlooked.[6]

But there was a *theological* explanation.

God didn't want the king to do anything until just the right time. That time would come later in *Esther 6*, when Haman almost succeeds in his demon-inspired plot to kill God's people. Only then will the Lord bring Mordecai's heroic deed back to the king's mind—and at just the moment the devil thinks he's won the day.

God was moving the chess pieces on the chess board of human history exactly when and where He wanted them. And He would eventually move this entire contest to a checkmate against the Kingdom of Darkness.[7]

That's the good news . . . but it's four chapters away.

So let's get back to the bad news.

MORDECAI'S DISOBEDIENT POSTURE

Instead of honoring or even promoting Mordecai, notice what the king does:

After these events, King Ahasuerus promoted Haman, the son of Hammedatha the Agagite, and advanced him and established his authority over all the princes who were with him. All the king's servants who were at the king's gate bowed down and paid homage to Haman; for so the king had commanded concerning him. But Mordecai neither bowed down nor paid homage (Esther 3:1-2).

We need to understand that this was more than just refusing to curtsy. In fact, whenever these two Hebrew verbs for bowing and paying homage are combined in the Old Testament, they always refer to worshiping and reverencing God.[8]

You can almost feel the tension rising, can't you? Mordecai had jeopardized everything he'd gained so far by refusing to bow.

But why risk all that now?

I've read several different views from Old Testament scholars on why Mordecai refused to bow to Haman:

- he was arrogant and upset that he wasn't promoted instead of Haman;
- he wasn't interested in court politics;
- he didn't like Haman;
- he enjoyed irritating Haman, who wanted everybody to treat him like a little god.

While there might be truth in all these opinions, the most important reason Mordecai refused to bow is found in ***Esther 3:4***. We don't even have to guess—Scripture tells us clearly that when the king's servants asked Mordecai why he wouldn't bow, he told them it was because he was a Jew.

So Mordecai wasn't simply refusing to follow Persian protocol. He was reacting to the fact that Haman wanted people to basically worship the ground he walked on. A faithful Jew would *never* give that kind of reverence to anyone but God, and Mordecai wouldn't either.

Wait . . . what's happened to Mordecai?

Isn't this the same Mordecai who refused to go back to Jerusalem? Isn't this the same Jew who sent his adopted daughter into a pagan harem and told her to keep her nationality a secret?

The same.

Then what's gotten into him? For five years he had been keeping his heritage a secret and made Esther swear to keep it secret, as well. "We can't let anybody know we're Jews . . . that'll hurt your chances for the crown and my chances at a career."

Now, all of a sudden, he leaks it to the press; but why *now*, after he had finally arrived and made a name for himself?

Why would he sacrifice his standing and reputation—and salary—at that particular moment? Not to mention Esther's safety and personal reputation. People knew Mordecai raised her. He was part of the celebration when she won the crown; his own career path benefited because of her. He now potentially exposed *her* secret, as well.

Fortunately, God blinded Haman's eyes to Mordecai's and Esther's kinship. Had he realized it then, he would have tried to assassinate the queen before passing his edict. But he missed it. He didn't connect the dots until it was too late . . . and his oversight would cost him his life.

There can only be a couple of reasons why Mordecai waited until that moment to reveal his identity.

- **He discovered how insignificant all the other stuff really was.**

He was the proverbial man who climbed the ladder of success all the way to the top only to discover that it was leaning against the wrong wall. His plate was full . . . but his heart was empty. He had everything just long enough to know none of it satisfied.

I recently talked to a member of Colonial Baptist Church who reminded me how God had brought Him to faith in Christ.

He told me, "Stephen, I had a great career . . . I had plenty of money . . . I had everything, but it felt like nothing . . . I was empty. So I began searching for spiritual truth."

He then explained how he had decided to try to find a church that taught directly from the Bible. Though he was raised Roman Catholic, he visited both Catholic and Protestant churches . . . dozens of them. But he couldn't find one that spoke directly from the Bible.

When he decided to visit Colonial, he saw the congregation and their pastor with their Bibles open and he was struck with the thought, *They're actually studying the Bible.* He laughed and told me that a sweet lady behind him noticed he was visiting and struck up a conversation with him. She asked him a few questions and invited him back. He found out a few months later that sweet lady was my wife Marsha.

Several weeks after his first visit, he prayed the sinner's prayer along with me as I closed the morning worship service, receiving Jesus Christ as his own personal Lord and Savior.

He was no longer empty . . . he now had what *mattered*.

Mordecai had been in the palace for at least four years now. He had a private office down the hall from the king. He had servants and prestige and power, and his adopted daughter was the queen of Persia.

He had everything . . . but it felt like nothing.

Maybe that's your story, too. You find yourself muttering under your breath, *There's gotta be something else . . . something more . . . something different.*

Mordecai knew what he needed to do. He was running from the true and living God—the God of Abraham and Isaac and Jacob.

He had seen enough to know that there must be a greater kingdom than the kingdom of Persia. Frankly, he'd come to understand that Persia was a mess. It was a kingdom led by an emotionally adolescent king who accomplished nothing more than adding to his harem and palace compound.

Life had become one great disappointment.

One author put it so well when he wrote, "Disappointment is the nurse of wisdom."[9]

Mordecai knew what mattered and, for the first time in this book, he wasn't ashamed to reveal it.

So that might be the first reason Mordecai decided to tell his secret.

- **The second was that he knew that to reverence anyone but God was to break God's law.**

In other words, he decided to finally take a stand for the Word of God. No wonder J. Vernon McGee wrote, "At this point in the story, I'm ready to throw my hat in the air and say, "Hurray for Mordecai. For the first time, he is taking a stand for God—and it will cost him potentially everything."[10]

Every time Haman, the hot shot, strutted through the gate and into the presidential office, everyone bowed. Up to this point, Mordecai must have found creative ways to keep from bowing. Maybe he slipped into the restroom whenever Haman came in, or perhaps he bent over the water fountain to get a drink at the moment of obeisance.

But no longer.

Mordecai wasn't going to hide anymore. As Haman's familiar chariot pulled up to the gate and the bowing began, Mordecai set his jaw. Literally and figuratively speaking, he was the last man standing.

HAMAN'S DEATH PROCLAMATION

When Haman saw that Mordecai neither bowed down nor paid homage to him, Haman was filled with rage. But he disdained to lay hands on Mordecai alone, for they had told him who the people of Mordecai were; therefore Haman sought to destroy all the Jews, the people of Mordecai, who were throughout the whole kingdom of Ahasuerus (Esther 3:5-6).

As far as Haman was concerned, Mordecai's disrespect presented the perfect opportunity to settle the old family feud, once and for all.

And he didn't want the life of one Jew . . . he wanted to eradicate every single Jew living throughout the kingdom—which, by the way, included Jerusalem.[11]

So Haman sought the counsel of his gods to find out what to do next.

In the first month, which is the month Nisan, in the twelfth year of King Ahasuerus, Pur, that is the lot, was cast before Haman from day to day and from month to month, until the twelfth month, that is the month Adar (Esther 3:7).

This lot was cast to discover the best date for exterminating the Jewish people. The date was *the thirteenth day of the twelfth month, which is the month Adar* (Esther 3:13*b*).

By the way, Haman was the only one in this story, so far, asking his god for advice on what to do next. And according to Persian custom, he had all the voodoo doctors come over and cast the *Pur* to determine the will of the gods.

The word *Pur* is the Akkadian word for stone. The stones were usually made from baked clay and shaped like modern dice, marked on all six sides, and cast out from a bowl.[12]

So Haman rolled the dice and they happened to land on the thirteenth day of Adar . . . and, it just so happened, that day was an incredibly significant day for the Jews. It marked the day before they would celebrate Passover as a nation to remember how God delivered them from slavery in Egypt 900 years earlier.

The Jews were about to get an unforgettable reminder that God wasn't just a Savior in the past . . . He was a Savior in the present.

Haman was throwing dice in his living room, and he thought his lucky number just turned up. But he failed to read Solomon's words that **the lot is cast into the lap, but its every decision is from the LORD** (Proverbs 16:33).

God even determines the roll of the dice. He's going to bring about a miracle on that particular day so He can provoke their memory—their conscience—and move their hearts back into fellowship with Him.

Even though the hand of God is invisible, the grace of God is unmistakable. God's redemption would be the clear providence of a gracious Redeemer.

But the storm clouds still gathered . . . a death warrant would be signed into law.

Notice how clever Haman was as he approached the king:

> *Then Haman said to King Ahasuerus, "There is a certain people scattered and dispersed among the peoples in all the provinces of your kingdom; their laws are different from those of all other people and they do not observe the king's laws, so it is not in the King's interest to let them remain"* (Esther 3:8).

Haman obviously knew which buttons to push. Remember that the king was still feeling the pain from Vashti's rebellion, two military defeats at the hands of the Greeks, and the attempted assassination by two of his trusted officers.[13]

Haman knew the king was in a vulnerable state, so he floated the thought that the slightest hint of rebellion must be stamped out—immediately.

But that wasn't all he proposed to the king. He sweetened the pot even more when he promised to pay the king ***10,000 talents of silver*** (Esther 3:9*b*) when the genocide was carried out. That's nearly 400 tons of silver—worth millions in today's economy.

But where in the world would Haman get that kind of money?

The Jews.

In the same way that the Third Reich amassed wealth during World War II by stripping the Jews of their assets and possessions, Haman would make Persia wealthier by plundering the Jews.

The king's response was a little odd, because he said to Haman,

> ***"The silver is yours, and the people also, to do with them as you please"*** (Esther 3:11).

Scholars, however, confirm this was just Middle Eastern posturing. In fact, we find out later in ***Esther 4*** that the King *did* expect to be paid in silver.

So the deal was struck and the edict was sent throughout the kingdom. The Jews were going to die on the eve of their Passover.

There were no loopholes in this edict, either. The king made his intentions clear:

> ***And letters were sent by couriers to all the king's provinces to destroy, to kill and to annihilate all the Jews, both young and old, women and children, in one day—the thirteenth day of the twelfth month, which is the month Adar, and to seize their possessions as plunder*** (Esther 3:13).

While the entire kingdom was told to get ready for the day of slaughter, the King of Darkness was wringing his hands in delight—the Jews escaped Egypt, but they would not escape Persia.

Haman's deception had worked. You can just picture the prime minister standing behind the king, whispering in his ear, "Listen, Ahasuerus, the Jews don't belong here. They're not like us. They're a threat to you because they really follow a different leader. They're in our way. Let's just get rid of them."

The Jewish people in Persia would be marginalized and treated with suspicion . . . friendships would end . . . Jewish businesses would fold. God's people would first be avoided and feared, hated and envied and, finally, killed.

Two thousand, four hundred years later during World War II, tactics from the same playbook were set in motion.

SATAN'S DELIBERATE PLAN

On the evening of November 9, 1938, a spontaneous eruption of violence against Jews occurred. Instigated primarily by Nazi party officials, the pogrom (ethnic cleansing) occurred throughout Germany, Austria, and a region of Czechoslovakia. The riots became known as *Kristallnacht* (German: Night of Broken Glass) because of the shattering of the windows of Jewish shops, stores, and homes.[14]

Fires across the country devoured synagogues and Jewish institutions. By the end of the rampage, gangs of Nazi storm troopers had destroyed 7,000 Jewish businesses, set fire to more than 900 synagogues, killed 91 Jews, and deported some 30,000 Jewish men to concentration camps.

Tension had been mounting. The Jewish people had been marginalized for months. Whispers circulated throughout Germany: Jews are different . . . they're a threat to the country . . . they're in the way of progress.

Himmler echoed the words of Hitler when he said of the Jews, "They do not belong to the same species but only imitate humans—they are as far removed from us as animals are from humans."[15]

And as Hitler's troops marched against the Jews, they chanted these unthinkable lyrics:

> Sharpen the long knives on the pavement stone;
> Sink the knives into Jewish flesh and bone,
> Let the blood flow freely.[16]

Where does that kind of hatred and violence originate? It didn't start in the heart of Himmler or Hitler . . . nor in the heart of Haman or Ahasuerus.

It originated in the heart of the King of Darkness.

Satan is the ultimate Jew-hater. His last gasp of defiance against God is found in *Revelation 20*, where he will bring to Jerusalem a final holocaust. There's a reason why the pages of history are stained with the blood of the Jew.

While God works in mysterious ways, Satan doesn't. His message is always the same, and his methods are always predictable.

He hates the thought of a Jewish Messiah. He hates the fact that God will keep the covenant He made with Abraham, Isaac, and Jacob. He hates the idea of redemption. So he battles on against God and His people.

Haman, Hitler, and their like have come and gone. But the real genius behind their genocidal plots still stalks the earth—and the family feud is alive and well. Satan merely found his puppets throughout history and goaded them into mounting offensives against the citizens of God's covenant nation.

That's why it's revealing to see how plugged in Hitler was to the occult. He hated Jesus Christ and the Church.

In Erwin Lutzer's courageous book *Hitler's Cross*, he digs into historical records and reveals just how deeply Hitler was involved with Satan.

According to Lutzer's research, Hitler's dance with the devil started in the Hofberg Library in Vienna. There was a spear in a display case mounted on the wall, which was said to be the spear that pierced Christ's side at the cross. Hitler was in his early twenties when he first saw the spear while taking a tour of the library. He overheard the guide say, "This spear is shrouded in mystery; whoever unlocks its secrets will rule the world."

Those words would change Hitler's life. He stood before the spear that very day and vowed to follow Satan. He went to that library and stared at the spear for hours, inviting its hidden powers to invade his soul. He believed this ancient weapon was a bridge between the natural world and the spiritual world.

Walter Stein, a friend of Hitler in those days, said that Hitler would stand before that spear "like a man in a trance or a man over whom some dreadful spell had been cast." He went on to say that "the very space around him seemed enlivened with some kind of ghostly light. He appeared transformed as if some mighty spirit now inhabited his very soul, creating within and around him an evil transformation."[17]

What else could account for Hitler's mesmerizing sway over the masses? What else could make world leaders tremble at the sight of him? He had given himself to the devil. He had been transformed with a demonic passion . . . he was just another Haman.

When Hitler eventually marched victoriously into Vienna, he went into that library, took down the spear for himself and claimed, "I am now holding the whole world in my hands."[18]

He almost did.

But he, too, would fail to become Satan's final antichrist. He would lose the war against the world and God's people.

Hitler would hear, as Haman heard centuries earlier, the whisper of divine Providence saying, "Checkmate."

Checkmate!

God moves kings as easily has He moves pawns. He owns all the chess pieces. In fact, He owns the chess board. He owns the table on which it sits—in every nation. And He owns the land upon which the table stands.

Mankind moves to do its will, but in the end the movements have ultimately accomplished *God's* will.

GOD'S DISTINCT PROVISION

So what was God really up to in ancient Persia? He was preparing His people to remember that even in Persia, He was sovereign.

He was bringing the Jewish people back to the moral of the story. . . they wouldn't find help in the government or in their friends; they wouldn't find security in their bank accounts or possessions; they wouldn't be able to hide at work . . . or at home . . . or anywhere in Persia.

They would be driven to the point of realizing that there was nothing at all that they could do to save themselves.

And that was exactly where God wanted them—He alone would be their refuge and their strong tower.

In June of 1937, a German pastor named Niemoller bravely preached against the atheism of the Third Reich, using these words to his congregation:

> We have no more thought of using our own powers to escape the authorities than the apostles of old. No more are we ready to keep silent at man's request when God commands us to speak. For it is, and must remain, the case that we must obey God rather than man.

Within a few days, Dr. Niemoller was arrested and imprisoned. He was held for seven months in solitary confinement before facing his trial on February 7, 1938. The indictments against him were fourteen pages long. He was accused of speaking against the Reich with malicious and provocative criticism. He had violated the law and was charged with "Abuse of Pulpit."

That day, a uniformed soldier arrived to escort Niemoller from his cell to the courtroom. As they made their way through the corridors of the prison and a long underground tunnel, this faithful pastor became overwhelmed with thoughts of loneliness and fear.

He knew that his trial held a foregone conclusion. But what he didn't know was why no one had sent word to him. Where were his family and friends? Where was his church that had stood with him?

He had heard from no one—they had been forbidden to communicate with him while he languished in solitary confinement.

With these thoughts flooding his mind, something remarkable happened. The soldier, whose face had thus far been impassive and who had not uttered a word, began to quietly speak, though still looking straight ahead.

His voice was so soft that Niemoller couldn't understand his words at first. But as they reverberated over and over along the walls of a tunnel, he was able to make them out: ***The name of the LORD is a strong tower; the righteous runs into it and is safe*** (Proverbs 18:10).

As Niemoller climbed the steps to the courtroom, he gave no sign that he had heard the words. But his fear was gone. A new sense of hope and trust took its place. He was condemned by the Third Reich and sent to a concentration camp for seven years. But he survived and was liberated at the end of the war to tell his story.[19]

Like Niemoller, the generation of Israelites in Persia were set to walk through the darkest and most terrifying tunnel of their lives. But they, too, would discover ***the name of the Lord is a strong tower; the righteous runs into it and is safe*** (Proverbs 18:10).

- When everyone else is unjust, He isn't.
- When everyone else gives up, He doesn't.
- When no one seems to notice, He does.
- When no one seems to care, He always will.
- Even when God seems distant, He is present.
- Even when God seems removed . . . He remains sovereign and faithful.

Perhaps that's exactly the lesson God wants you to learn—all over again . . . today.

So what was God doing in ***Esther 3***? He was moving the chess pieces of history so His people would once again discover that He alone was their strong tower.

Act IV is about to begin!

When Mordecai learned all that had been done, he tore his clothes, put on sackcloth and ashes, and went out into the midst of the city and wailed loudly and bitterly. ²And he went as far as the king's gate, for no one was to enter the king's gate clothed in sackcloth. ³And in each and every province where the command and decree of the king came, there was great mourning among the Jews, with fasting, weeping, and wailing; and many lay on sackcloth and ashes. ⁴Then Esther's maidens and her eunuchs came and told her, and the queen writhed in great anguish. And she sent garments to clothe Mordecai that he might remove his sackcloth from him, but he did not accept them. ⁵Then Esther summoned Hathach from the king's eunuchs, whom the king had appointed to attend her, and ordered him to go to Mordecai to learn what this was and why it was. ⁶So Hathach went out to Mordecai to the city square in front of the king's gate. ⁷And Mordecai told him all that had happened to him, and the exact amount of money that Haman had promised to pay to the king's treasuries for the destruction of the Jews. ⁸He also gave him a copy of the text of the edict which had been issued in Susa for their destruction, that he might show Esther and inform her, and to order her to go in to the king to implore his favor and to plead with him for her people. ⁹And Hathach came back and related Mordecai's words to Esther. ¹⁰Then Esther spoke to Hathach and ordered him to reply to Mordecai: ¹¹"All the king's servants and the people of the king's provinces know that for any man or woman who comes to the king to the inner court who is not summoned, he has but one law, that he be put to death, unless the king holds out to him the golden scepter so that he may live. And I have not been summoned to come to the king for these thirty days." ¹²And they related Esther's words to Mordecai. ¹³Then Mordecai told them to reply to Esther, "Do not imagine that you in the king's palace can escape any more than all the Jews. ¹⁴For if you remain silent at this time, relief and deliverance will arise for the Jews from another place and you and your father's house will perish. And who knows whether you have not attained royalty for such a time as this?" ¹⁵Then Esther told them to reply to Mordecai, ¹⁶"Go, assemble all the Jews who are found in Susa, and fast for me; do not eat or drink for three days, night or day. I and my maidens also will fast in the same way. And thus I will go in to the king, which is not according to the law; and if I perish, I perish." ¹⁷So Mordecai went away and did just as Esther had commanded him.

—Esther 4

CHAPTER FIVE

DEFINING MOMENTS

Esther 4

GOD'S DETERMINATION

A little girl was born into slavery in Dorchester County, Maryland, in 1822. Her nights in the slave quarters were most often cold, and she slept as close to the fire as possible. Sometimes she even stuck her toes into the smoldering ashes to avoid frostbite.

By the age of six, she was considered old enough to work all day and was hired out to temporary masters, some who were cruel and negligent. That lasted just until she was caught stealing a sugar cube; the mistress of the house whipped her and sent her back home.

While working as a field hand as a young teen, she was injured by a blow to her head from an iron weight, thrown by an angry overseer at a fleeing slave. The severe injury resulted in occasional seizures and headaches for the rest of her life.

When she was 27 years old, her owner died, leaving her and her family at risk of being sold to pay his debts. Late in the fall of 1849, she tapped into an Underground Railroad that was already functioning well on the Eastern Shore: traveling by night, using the North Star and instructions from white and black helpers, she found her way to Philadelphia. She had escaped the chains of slavery.

But that didn't end her problems. In fact, she later described upon arriving, "I had crossed the line and I was free, but there was no one to welcome me to the land of freedom. I was a stranger in a strange land."[1]

She sought work as a domestic, saving her money to help the rest of her family escape. From 1850 to 1860, the woman conducted at least eleven escape missions, aiding approximately seventy individuals, including her brothers, parents, and other family and friends, while also giving instructions to fifty more who found their way to freedom independently.

She would devote the rest of her life to rescuing slaves from the South and leading them to free states in the North.

Her name was Harriet Tubman.

Considered one of the most fearless conductors along what was known as the Underground Railroad, Tubman was known only by the complimentary nickname Moses.

But before Harriet ever became a hero to the western world, she was first an outlaw. So much so, in fact, that rewards were posted throughout Maryland offering $50,000 for her capture—the equivalent of nearly one million dollars today.

Tubman was hunted on numerous occasions by professional gunmen, dogs, and even wild animals, but she managed to elude them all. And in spite of their constant pursuit, she continued to fulfill her mission of rescuing slaves. She determined to fight for their freedom as long as she had strength, and she sincerely believed that when it came time for her to go, God would let her be captured.[2]

Harriet's abiding sense of calling and purpose compelled her to eventually lead more than a thousand slaves to freedom.

Throughout the Civil War she provided badly needed nursing care to black soldiers and hundreds of newly liberated slaves who crowded Union camps. Tubman's military service expanded to include spying and scouting behind Confederate lines.

When an early biography was being written about her, Frederick Douglass, a former slave who became a well-respected entrepreneur and abolitionist, was asked to write words of commendation on her life. Instead, he penned these stirring words to Harriett in a letter dated August 29, 1868:

> I need words of commendation from you more than you need them from me, especially where your superior labors and devotion to the cause of the lately enslaved of our land are known as I know them. The difference between us is very marked. Most that I have done and

suffered in the service of our cause has been in public, and I have received encouragement at every step of the way. You, on the other hand, have labored in a private way. I have wrought in the day—you in the night. I have had the applause of the crowd and the satisfaction that comes of being approved by the multitude, while the most that you have done has been witnessed by a few trembling, scarred, and foot-sore bondmen and women, whom you have led out of the house of bondage, and whose heartfelt *"God bless you"* has been your only reward. The midnight sky and the silent stars have been the witnesses of your devotion and I know of no other who willingly encountered more perils and hardships to serve our people than you have.[3]

There is little surprise that to this day Harriet Tubman is revered and honored for her self-sacrificing efforts for the freedom and safety of her fellow slaves.

That kind of biography should inspire us to live for something greater than ourselves, no matter what the cost—which is exactly why **Esther 4** is such an incredible portion of Scripture.

At this point, Esther begins her own biography of heroism and sacrifice, redefining her resolve, purpose, mission, and lifestyle.

King Ahasuerus had only recently allowed the plans to be put into place to annihilate the Jewish people. Posters were put up throughout Persia, informing the kingdom of the date of the coming genocide.

This wasn't a secret endeavor. It was a national affair and *everyone* would be expected to participate. The message was simple and straightforward: *every Jew must die.*

Furthermore, the Persians could pillage the victims' homes and steal their possessions before Haman got his hands on anything. There was blood money to be had.

No doubt many Persian men and women circled the date on their calendar and made plans to strike early . . . plans to get rich overnight.

Inside the king's palace, unknown and unseen, God was at work unfolding His own plans—the rescue of the enslaved Jewish people.

Up to this point, Esther had managed to keep her heritage a secret for nearly five years. Perhaps she thought she could get away with it forever. She was wrong. Her secret began to unravel bit by bit as God's plans continued to unfold.

The king's prime minister had already discovered that Mordecai was a Jew but, fortunately, he failed to see Mordecai's familial tie to Esther. He was still bitter and outraged by Mordecai's refusal to bow to him; he was licking his chops in anticipation of that day when he would end the longstanding family feud once and for all. He knew Mordecai wouldn't be alive much longer, and that thought brought him great pleasure.

It's important to note here that those who cast off the Book of Esther because it never mentions the name of God fail to see that it also never mentions the name of Satan.[4] Both, however, are obviously at work in this story. One is pulling the strings . . . the other is about to be strung up.

Esther 4 provides us with yet another account of Satan's assault on God's people. He will do whatever he can to ensure that the Messiah never steps foot on earth, which means he must get rid of the Jewish people . . . all of them.

And Satan had every reason to believe he'd succeed. But as he sat back and waited for the coming carnage, he and his puppet Haman overlooked the most important player on the chess board: the queen.

Perhaps he thought of Esther as a lucky orphan girl who made it to the winner's circle—just another pretty face in the royal harem.

Or perhaps he knew she was related to Mordecai and assumed that Esther didn't care to be numbered among them. After all, she had forsaken her identity long ago and had kept it hidden for five years. Moreover, she had disobeyed God by marrying a Gentile—an idolater, at that.

Maybe the devil had simply forgotten how little time it takes for God to change a person's heart.

In the meantime, Esther was steadily rising to prominence in the king's court. She *happened* to win the most coveted seat in his palace. She *happened* to be the cousin of Mordecai, who *happened* to be given an administrative position in the king's court. And because of that privileged position, Mordecai *happened* to uncover a plot against the king—which made him a hero and ultimately would save his life . . . not to mention the fact that Esther and Mordecai *happened* to be Jews and part of God's remnant.

The world would look at this story and say, "Wow, what an amazing string of coincidences." But we read this story and say, "Wow, what an amazing God."

But these are not coincidences. In fact, there is no such thing as a coincidence. A coincidence is a feeble explanation for God's work behind the scenes. Coincidences are the providential acts of God, Who prefers to remain anonymous.[5]

Defining moments, then, are those moments when we recognize the acts of God—the flickering shadows of His hand in life—and we surrender, even partner with Him, as He plays out His purposes.

God doesn't just have plans . . . He has plans *for us*. Whether it's rescuing slaves or risking the crown, God has a purpose which sweeps us into His daily drama.

In Act IV, these four scenes demonstrate that concept in living color—and in dramatic fashion.

SCENE I: MORDECAI'S DEMONSTRATION

Just outside the administrative offices,

When Mordecai learned all that had been done, he tore his clothes, put on sackcloth and ashes, and went out into the midst of the city and wailed loudly and bitterly. And he went as far as the king's gate, for no one was to enter the king's gate clothed in sackcloth (Esther 4:1-2).

So there was Mordecai—his heritage recently revealed—identifying with the Jewish people who are now headed for certain death. No more hiding. No more trying to impress the administrative office. He is now weeping with the Jews . . . for the Jews . . . as a Jew.[6]

In our Western world we do a pretty good job of hiding our tears behind handkerchiefs and sunglasses. But Middle Easterners aren't like that. If you've ever seen footage from that part of the world—perhaps after the death of a family member or a supposed martyr—you see men walking with a casket over their heads through a mob of wailing people.[7]

That's exactly what's happening here. Mordecai was dressed in dark, coarse clothing made of goat hair (similar to burlap) to demonstrate his preoccupation with pain.[8]

He ripped his clothing as a symbol of the tearing of his emotions and his broken heart. He also rubbed ashes onto his head and beard, a custom for Jews who were begging God either for repentance or deliverance.[9] What a sight this must have been for those passing by.

But those actions alone don't prove that Mordecai was finally getting his heart right with God. He was grieving all right, but he wasn't the only one.

> *And in each and every province where the command and decree of the king came, there was great mourning among the Jews, with fasting, weeping, and wailing; and many lay on sackcloth and ashes* (Esther 4:3).

While the individual words for *fasting, weeping, and wailing* appear many times in the Old Testament, this appearance in *Esther 4* is unique and incredibly significant. In fact, the only other time in the Hebrew Bible where you find these three verbs in exactly that identical construction is in *Joel 2:12*.

I agree with many Hebrew scholars who see this reference as a direct parallel to Joel's prophecy. The original readers would have immediately connected Ezra's construction here with Joel's invitation, *"Yet even now,"* declares the LORD, *"return to Me with all your heart, and with fasting, weeping, and mourning"* (Joel 2:12).

Mordecai had actually experienced the first spiritually defining moment in his life. He no longer kept to his hidden agenda. He was helpless to save himself. He was effectively revealing which God he belonged to, in plain sight of every Persian who passed by the palace, while challenging every Jew to join him in crying out to God for help.

Those were not the tears of great depression . . . they were tears of great revival.

Later, in *Esther 4:16*, Queen Esther will follow Mordecai's example and ask him to have all the Jews in Susa fast for her . . . but she's not quite there yet.

SCENE II: ESTHER'S HESITATION

When Esther heard that Mordecai was dressed in sackcloth, she actually sent him a new suit of clothes and asked him to change into them. When he refused, Esther sent her personal eunuch to find out what his problem was *(Esther 4:5)*.

She was evidently sequestered inside the queen's quarters and had some-how remained ignorant of what was going on outside the palace. But she heard a rumor from someone that Mordecai was dressed in rags, weeping and wailing, outside the palace offices. Esther didn't know what was wrong; in fact, it's possible that she didn't yet know about the edict.

When Mordecai refused her gift of clothing, she sent her personal attendant and bodyguard Hathach to find out why. He soon returned with a copy of the edict and delivered to her the frightful news that her people are going to be massacred. Hathach was, most likely, one of the few people who knew Esther was a Jewess; there's a strong possibility he may have been a Jew himself.

But if that news wasn't bad enough for Esther, Hathach went on to inform her that Mordecai had asked her to ***go in to the King to implore his favor and to plead with him for her people*** (Esther 4:8*b*).

Her face must have turned deathly pale. Mordecai couldn't be serious . . . could he? No one knew these were her people. She'd kept her secret hidden from the king and his advisors. Only her most trusted friends and personal staff would have known, if anyone did. Besides, even if she wanted to let people know she was a Jew, two massive obstacles stood in the way of her being able to save them.

1. **A legal problem:** Esther sent Hathach back to Mordecai to remind him of something he'd obviously forgotten in his depressed state of mind. She said:

   "All the king's servants and the people of the king's provinces know that for any man or woman who comes to the king to the inner court who is not summoned, he has but one law, that he be put to death, unless the king holds out to him the golden scepter so that he may live" (Esther 4:11).

Nobody just walks into the Oval Office. That would be suicide . . . even for a queen. And just remember what happened to the *last* queen who disobeyed Ahazuerus' orders. Esther certainly hadn't forgotten.

2. **A personal problem:** Esther added this little fact:

   "I have not been summoned to come to the king for these thirty days" (Esther 4:11*b*).

Many Old Testament scholars read into this that Ahasuerus' interest in Esther was waning. It seemed that Esther's hold on the king's favor was slipping, while the king's harem continued growing.

There's an old saying that when you marry a child of the devil, you will eventually run into problems with your father-in-law.[10]

So as far as Esther was concerned, the timing for the king's decree against the Jewish people couldn't be worse. What a predicament; the devil's plans have her cornered. If she remained silent, the edict would be carried out and surely someone—perhaps even Mordecai—would spill the beans. But if she interceded before the king on behalf of her people, she'd be admitting her heritage that she'd kept secret from him the past five years.

Ahazuerus thought Esther was Persian. It had already been difficult enough for him that she wasn't related to any of the seven noble families from which, according to Persian custom, the queen was supposed to come. Now he stood to face incredible humiliation and embarrassment for the fact that he had actually ordered the death of the queen's own people . . . and his queen, too.

Frankly, he would look like an idiot.

And if the previous chapters of this story have taught us anything about this king, he didn't want to look like a fool. If in doubt, anyone could ask the former queen and she would tell them that he's not the kind of man you want to publically embarrass.

3. **A communication problem:** This was another obstacle that many people overlook. If a person had a petition for the king, the business had to first be communicated to the supreme commander—the king's prime minister—who arranged the appointments on the basis of priority . . . and that supreme commander was Haman. Esther would have to communicate her secret to him before it ever reached the ears of the king . . . and she certainly couldn't give her secret away to Haman.[11]

All these things were stacked in favor of Haman. Esther didn't stand a chance at gaining the upper hand against the king's most trusted associate. Besides, Ahazuerus had seemingly lost interest in her.

So Esther did what many of us might have done—nothing.

Perhaps Mordecai anticipated her fear and hesitancy; no doubt, he recognized the impossibility of her situation. Interceding before the king was a long shot, and he knew it. But while he was mourning in sackcloth and ashes outside the palace, he formulated a divinely inspired challenge to Esther that would change everything.

When Hathach came back to deliver Esther's refusal, Mordecai gave him an amazing message to take to the queen. Call it a motivational speech, call it oratory at its best, call it whatever you will—but it had the power to change Esther's mind and heart. The message can do the same for us today.

SCENE III: MORDECAI'S CONFRONTATION

Then Mordecai told them to reply to Esther, "Do not imagine that you in the king's palace can escape any more than all the Jews" (Esther 4:13).

Several incentives, so to speak, are bundled up in his message. Here's the first one: "The palace walls can't save you. Don't even think for a moment that you're gonna be safe while the Jews are massacred in every province. You can't hide behind the curtains in your apartment, and you can't hide under the crown on your head. This is a reality check, Esther—if the Jews die, you'll die as well. So you might as well admit who you are now."

It may be a form of literary irony that, at the beginning of this story, Scripture gives us two names for this queen: Hadassah, (her Hebrew name) and Esther (her Persian name). Now, at this juncture in the story, the queen would have to decide which name she was going to live out. Mordecai had confronted her with the question, "Just who are you . . . Hebrew or Persian?"

For Esther, her defining moment began with a question she'd been avoiding for years.

In my travels to other countries, I've had the privilege of meeting numerous believers who gave their birth name and their Christian name. They told me that they adopted a biblical name like Daniel or Jeremiah or Ruth at the time of their baptism. This decision became their new identity for the rest of their lives.

We can learn a lesson from those fellow believers, can't we?

We forget sometimes that we have two names as well. One is the name on our birth certificate; the other is the name given to us by our Savior. It identifies us as His—*Christian*.

Defining moments come into our own lives most often when we, like Esther, determine which name we're going to identify with.

Mordecai was reminding Esther who she really was.

But he didn't stop there; here comes the next one:

"For if you remain silent at this time, relief and deliverance will arise from the Jews from another place and you and your father's house will perish" (Esther 4:14*a*).

Just as she couldn't escape her true identity, she couldn't escape God's promise, either. Mordecai was reminding Esther who the *real* sovereign of Persia was.

He obviously had captured his own defining moment of faith and had cast his lot with God's people. His mourning had turned to confidence as he proclaimed his faith that God would send relief and deliverance somehow.

The Hebrew word *maqom*, translated *place* is a reference to God. Rabbis often referred to God as The Place.[12]

It's no wonder that Josephus and other Hebrew commentators over the last millennia have viewed this verse as a veiled allusion to God.[13]

Mordecai didn't know *what* God was planning, but he knew that God *was* planning. Most often, that's all our faith needs to know.

This was the faith of another Jew who hid in a cellar from the Nazis. He scribbled on the stone wall these defining words; "I believe in the sun even when it is not shining; I believe in God even when He is silent."[14]

Mordecai was in a dark place as well, but he believed God would keep His promise to Abraham, Isaac, and Jacob and deliver His people yet again. But just to make sure he got his point across to Esther, he threw in that little addendum about judgment. He basically said, "Esther, you can hide from everyone else inside these palace walls but you can't hide from God. If you're willing to let an entire nation be slaughtered just to save your own skin, God will surely punish you for it."

This was probably a hard truth for Esther to hear but one she definitely needed to consider. Still, Mordecai's most emphatic statement came next. Beyond the warning of judgment was the challenge of purpose—the final incentive:

"And who knows whether you have not attained royalty for such a time as this?" (Esther 4:14*b*).

"Can't you see it, Esther?" Mordecai exclaimed. "This is God's doing. That competition you won, that promotion I received . . . it was all part of God's master plan. He placed us here for this single purpose—to rescue His people."

Isn't that the greatest incentive we have for serving God today? It's not about fearing death and facing judgment; it's about God's use of us to accomplish His plans for the redemption of mankind. It's about our being willing and ready to say, "Yes, Lord, I want to be part of the work You're doing."

The call to discipleship is not just a call to surrender—it is an invitation to join the rescue efforts of God's Spirit throughout the world as the Father searches for those who will worship Him in spirit and in truth.

This is the exciting part of the mysterious synergy between God's sovereignty and man's cooperation. The same Lord who said, *"I will build my church and the gates of Hades shall not overpower it"* (Matthew 16:18), is the One who commanded His disciples to *"Go therefore and make disciples of all the nations, baptizing them in the name of the Father and the Son and the Holy Spirit, teaching them to observe all that I commanded you"* (Matthew 28:19-20*a*).

This is the truth that can redefine our lives. God is going to build His Church with or without us, but He is inviting us to join Him in His work.

He isn't going to come down here and teach that three-year-old Sunday school class. He isn't going to put money in the offering plate for ministry and building projects. He isn't going to write the curriculum for adult Bible studies or evangelize on a nearby campus.

He asks us to do that.

And when we join Him in that work, we witness profound things—not just in the lives of other people, but in our lives, as well.

Will you wash dishes at the local rescue mission for such a time as this? Will you take care of kids in the nursery for such a time as this? Will you publically identify with Jesus Christ at work for such a time as this?

Will you open your eyes and realize *your* life's greater purpose, as Mordecai saw his? God wants to use you. He has something in mind for you today . . . no matter how trivial or mundane. You represent Him. You are invited to join Him in the movement of His hand throughout the world.

I read three levels of motivation by Mordecai to Esther:

1. Take care of someone's physical concerns.
2. Give someone recognition and respect.
3. Give someone a sense of purpose and destiny.[15]

Esther may have been Queen of Persia, but it didn't matter in that moment. God gave her the crown—not so she could spend her life in luxury, power, ease, and wealth, but so she could use her influence to save her people.

Can you imagine how Mordecai's message must have struck her? Maybe it was the first time her mind flashed back to her life before the pageant, to the months of anticipation and preparation, to the day when the crown was placed on her head.

Maybe here, in this quiet reverie, she grasped for the first time what we, the readers, have understood on every page of this story so far: God was behind the scenes, and He was the One orchestrating the finale.

Mordecai was challenging Esther to make a decision that would change her life forever. "This is your hour, Esther—this is your defining moment. Stand. Speak. And perhaps even die. But whatever you do, do not remain silent."[16]

The last scene of this drama reveals her climactic response.

SCENE IV: ESTHER'S AFFIRMATION

Mordecai's message didn't fall on deaf ears. Esther not only responded affirmatively to his plea, but she began to put her own plan into action.

The first thing she did was summon the Jewish people to fast. She commanded Mordecai to **assemble all the Jews who are found in Susa, and fast for me; do not eat or drink for three days, night or day** (Esther 4:16*a*).

Esther was literally applying by faith this prophecy:

"Blow a trumpet in Zion, consecrate a fast, proclaim a solemn assembly" (Joel 2:15).

But she didn't stop there. The second statement she made publically affirmed her identity with God's people. She added,

"I and my maidens also will fast in the same way" (Esther 4:16*b*).

Many scholars believe that Esther had surrounded herself with Jewish servants and attendants out of sympathy and concern for them. For nearly five years they must have wondered why this Persian queen cared so much about Jewish people.

Now they knew . . . she was one of them.

Perhaps the greatest and most affirming aspect of Esther's plan, however, was that she finally surrendered to God's will:

"I will go in to the King, which is not according to the law; and if I perish, I perish" (Esther 4:16c).

What a change of heart.

She changed from fear to faith; from hesitation to determination; from concern about her own safety to concern for her people's survival.[17]

Like young David who looked at a giant on the battlefield and saw an opportunity to reveal God's power, Esther had finally come to recognize the great opportunity she has been given from the Lord.

As one author so poignantly stated, Esther had discovered that "there is no safety in a significant life . . . there is no significance in a safe life."[18]

This was her defining moment.

There are two things we need to understand about defining moments before we close the curtain on this dramatic chapter.

1. **Defining moments are those small steps of obedience that bring us closer to becoming the disciple God wants us to be.**

Douglas MacArthur once said that in the world there is a constant conspiracy against the brave: an age-old struggle between the roar of the crowd on one side and the voice of conscience on the other.

I'd like to amend that for the Christian disciple's defining moments: the struggle between the roar of the crowd on one side and the voice of *Christ* on the other.

For us, a defining moment will occur when we decide whether or not we will read the Word of God or bow our head to pray at the restaurant or, when asked what we did over the weekend, tell people we went to church.

Defining moments aren't usually all that dramatic. They are, instead, small, simple steps of obedience where we live up to our name and obey the voice of Christ.

2. **Defining moments are those small steps of faith where we trust God the way He deserves to be trusted.**

Eugene Peterson, known for his paraphrase of the Bible called *The Message*, wrote these words about Esther:

> The moment Haman surfaced, Esther began to move from being a beauty queen to becoming a [believer]; from being an empty-headed sex symbol to being a passionate intercessor; from the busy life in the harem to the high-risk venture of speaking for and identifying with the people of God.[19]

Esther needed to start living like that because God deserved to be trusted like that. And He still does today.

So what will we do with the defining moments that come into our lives? Whose name will we identify with?

The slave woman made the decision one night to run for her life and her freedom. That defining moment led to another and yet another, until, years later Harriet "Moses" Tubman became a household name and a national example of courage.

The difference between a hero and another human being is the voice they listen to. Most listen for the affirmation of the crowd. A true hero listens to the voice of conscience . . . ultimately, the voice of Christ.

Take a stand today. Speak out for what is right. Identify with your Savior. Partner with the movement of God's invisible hand.

You are *who* you are and *where* you are for such a time as this . . . make the most of it.

Now it came about on the third day that Esther put on her royal robes and stood in the inner court of the king's palace in front of the king's rooms, and the king was sitting on his royal throne in the throne room, opposite the entrance to the palace. [2] And it happened when the king saw Esther the queen standing in the court, she obtained favor in his sight; and the king extended to Esther the golden scepter which was in his hand. So Esther came near and touched the top of the scepter. [3] Then the king said to her, "What is troubling you, Queen Esther? And what is your request? Even to half of the kingdom it will be given to you." [4] And Esther said, "If it please the king, may the king and Haman come this day to the banquet that I have prepared for him." [5] Then the king said, "Bring Haman quickly that we may do as Esther desires." So the king and Haman came to the banquet which Esther had prepared. [6] And, as they drank their wine at the banquet, the king said to Esther, "What is your petition, for it shall be granted to you. And what is your request? Even to half of the kingdom it shall be done." [7] So Esther answered and said, "My petition and my request is: [8] if I have found favor in the sight of the king, and if it please the king to grant my petition and do what I request, may the king and Haman come to the banquet which I shall prepare for them, and tomorrow I will do as the king says." [9] Then Haman went out that day glad and pleased of heart; but when Haman saw Mordecai in the king's gate, and that he did not stand up or tremble before him, Haman was filled with anger against Mordecai. [10] Haman controlled himself, however, went to his house, and sent for his friends and his wife Zeresh. [11] Then Haman recounted to them the glory of his riches, and the number of his sons, and every instance where the king had magnified him, and how he had promoted him above the princes and servants of the king. [12] Haman also said, "Even Esther the queen let no one but me come with the king to the banquet which she had prepared; and tomorrow also I am invited by her with the king. [13] Yet all of this does not satisfy me every time I see Mordecai the Jew sitting at the king's gate." [14] Then Zeresh his wife and all his friends said to him, "Have a gallows fifty cubits high made and in the morning ask the king to have Mordecai hanged on it, then go joyfully with the king to the banquet." And the advice pleased Haman, so he had the gallows made.

–Esther 5:1-14

(Continued on next page)

(Continued)

During that night the king could not sleep so he gave an order to bring the book of records, the chronicles, and they were read before the king. [2]*And it was found written what Mordecai had reported concerning Bigthana and Teresh, two of the king's eunuchs who were doorkeepers, that they had sought to lay hands on King Ahasuerus.* [3]*And the king said, "What honor or dignity has been bestowed on Mordecai for this?" Then the king's servants who attended him said, "Nothing has been done for him."* [4]*So the king said, "Who is in the court?" Now Haman had just entered the outer court of the king's palace in order to speak to the king about hanging Mordecai on the gallows which he had prepared for him.* [5]*And the king's servants said to him, "Behold, Haman is standing in the court." And the king said, "Let him come in."* [6]*So Haman came in and the king said to him, "What is to be done for the man whom the king desires to honor?" And Haman said to himself, "Whom would the king desire to honor more than me?"* [7]*Then Haman said to the king, "For the man whom the king desires to honor,* [8]*let them bring a royal robe which the king has worn, and the horse on which the king has ridden, and on whose head a royal crown has been placed;* [9]*and let the robe and the horse be handed over to one of the king's most noble princes and let them array the man whom the king desires to honor and lead him on horseback through the city square, and proclaim before him, 'Thus it shall be done to the man whom the king desires to honor.'"* [10]*Then the king said to Haman, "Take quickly the robes and the horse as you have said, and do so for Mordecai the Jew, who is sitting at the king's gate; do not fall short in anything of all that you have said."* [11]*So Haman took the robe and the horse, and arrayed Mordecai, and led him on horseback through the city square, and proclaimed before him, "Thus it shall be done to the man whom the king desires to honor."* [12]*Then Mordecai returned to the king's gate. But Haman hurried home, mourning, with his head covered.* [13]*And Haman recounted to Zeresh his wife and all his friends everything that had happened to him. Then his wise men and Zeresh his wife said to him, "If Mordecai, before whom you have begun to fall, is of Jewish origin, you will not overcome him, but will surely fall before him."* [14]*While they were still talking with him, the king's eunuchs arrived and hastily brought Haman to the banquet which Esther had prepared.*

–Esther 6:1-14

CHAPTER SIX

ONCE UPON A SLEEPLESS NIGHT

Esther 5:1-6:14

GOD'S PROVIDENCE

Thomas Watson, a Puritan pastor in the seventeenth century, penned these profound words about God's providence:

> There is no such thing as blind fate, but there is a Providence that guides and governs the world. Providence is God's ordering all issues and events of things, after the counsel of His will, to His own glory. The wheels of the clock seem to move contrary one to the other, but they help forward the hands of the clock.

Another Puritan named Henry Law, who lived two centuries after Thomas Watson, wrote:

> No sparrow falls, no leaf decays, but in accordance with God's ordering mind. Chance is a figment of a dreaming pillow. Chance never was and it never can be. Thus, to the child of God there is no trifle or unimportant event. Momentous issues often hang on quick words, on sudden looks, on unintended steps.[1]

In light of what we will discover in this chapter, momentous issues also hang on unexpected invitations and sleepless nights in a king's palace.

God was at work behind every shadow . . . nothing had happened by chance. And Esther would finally discover that for herself, while the ink on the edict of death was barely dry.

Esther had promised Mordecai and the Jewish people at large that she would risk her life and confront the king about the death warrant he and Haman had set into motion.

She had called upon her people to fast for her, and the three-day fast was now completed. It was time for her to act. And when she did, some breathtaking twists and turns followed closely on the heels of her actions.

INVITATION OF A LIFETIME

Now it came about on the third day that Esther put on her royal robes and stood in the inner court of the king's palace in front of the king's rooms, and the king was sitting on his royal throne in the throne room, opposite the entrance to the palace. And it happened when the king saw Esther the queen standing in the court, she obtained favor in his sight (Esther 5:1-2a).

Okay . . . that was easy. Perhaps a bit too easy, which is why Bible scholars over the last few hundred years have puzzled over how quickly Esther received favor from the king in this passage. Why did Ahasuerus interrupt the business of his court and violate Persian protocol to hear Esther's request? After all, Esther had finished her message three days earlier with the words, "If I perish, I perish." She obviously wouldn't have expected this ready reception. You don't just waltz into the king's court and announce that your agenda is more important than his.

The Jewish scholars who translated the Old Testament into Greek (called the Septuagint, written a century before Jesus' birth) added their own commentary to the original text in an attempt to make this story a little more believable:

> Esther's heart was pounding with fear. When she had passed through all the doors, she stood before the king. Raising his face, flushed with color, he looked at her in fiercest anger. The queen stumbled, turned pale, and fainted. He sprang from his throne in alarm, and took her up in his arms until she revived and comforted her with reassuring words.[2]

Sounds more reasonable, I suppose . . . although it reminds me more of a fairytale. The truth is, while the genuine account is more cryptic, it's actually much more amazing.

Ezra tells us what really happened next:

And the king extended to Esther the golden scepter which was in his hand. So Esther came near and touched the top of the scepter. Then the king said to her, "What is troubling you, Queen Esther? And what is your request? Even to half of the kingdom it will be given to you" (Esther 5:2b-3).

Tilting the scepter toward Esther was court protocol for her *acceptance* before the king. The good news of the scepter was that instead of killing her, the king was allowing her to live.

An even greater surprise, of course, was that he didn't even rebuke her for the intrusion. She received not only the king's pardon but, evidently, a measure of respect.

All eyes were on Esther. The affairs of the palace court came to a sudden halt as the king invited Esther to step forward.

Recently, I went downtown to the courthouse to pay for a speeding ticket I'd received. After paying my fine, I slipped into a courtroom to say hello to a friend presiding over a case that day. Sitting on the front row was a group of six guys in orange jumpsuits, all of them shackled together. When I got up to leave, my friend motioned for me to come forward. I shook my head, not wanting to intrude, but he motioned and said, "Come here." I couldn't exactly say no to a judge. I walked down the aisle and went through that little swinging door past those six convicts. "How ya doing?" didn't seem to be appropriate.

Everything came to a halt as I made my way to the bench; every eye was on me—not exactly my most comfortable moment of the day.

Multiply that one moment of tension by a few thousand and you have a picture of what Esther was experiencing as she stood before the king.

Archeologists have confirmed that standing just below the throne of that Persian monarch would have been a man holding an axe in his hands. I thought six guys in orange jumpsuits and chains were a frightening sight. Can you imagine walking past an enormous guard with a battle-axe, whose job included executing intruders?.

Esther probably thought she was going to lose her head and, frankly, without the providence of God working on her behalf, she would have.

But the king surprised her and everyone else when he said instead,

"What is troubling you, Queen Esther? And what is your request? Even to half of the kingdom it will be given to you" (Esther 5:3).

The king basically told Esther that he was in the mood to give her anything she wanted.

She responded to him with a ready-made request:

"If it please the king, may the king and Haman come this day to the banquet that I have prepared for him" (Esther 5:4).

Her invitation, by the way, was a stroke of genius. By inviting Haman to come with the king, Esther knew it would quell any potential suspicions aroused in him. Haman should have asked himself why the queen had risked her life just to invite her husband to dinner. He should have suspected the queen was up to something and sought to discover what her secret was.

Instead, his ego was so inflated by having received that private invitation that those thoughts never even crossed his mind.

And don't miss the fact that there seemed to be a change of plans in Esther's strategy. She had informed Mordecai earlier that she intended to petition the king on behalf of her people after three days of fasting. Now was the time; it seemed that she would tell the king then and there. It was her opportunity . . . she'd gained access to his court.

This was her defining moment . . . but she didn't take it.

Evidently, during her days of fasting, God provoked in her thoughts and mind a *different* plan: one to lure the king and the conspirator away from the court, the press, and the public embarrassment that would naturally arise when the king discovered that his own hand had signed the death warrant of his favorite wife. He'd already lost one wife because of foolish decisions.

Esther's plan would provide privacy when her revelation was made to the king, making it much easier for him to change his mind and alter the death edict.

King Ahasuerus and Haman arrived for dinner and enjoyed a well-prepared meal. Afterward, he and Haman were having dessert, and the king said to Esther,

"What is your petition, for it shall be granted to you" (Esther 5:6*b*).

In other words, the king was smart enough to realize that Esther had something very important to ask of him—important enough to risk her life. So he basically told her to come out with it!

This was the moment Esther had been waiting for. She carefully replied:

***"My petition and my request is: if I have found favor in the sight
of the king, and if it please the king to grant my petition and do
what I request, may the king and Haman come to the banquet
which I shall prepare for them, and tomorrow I will do as the king
says"*** (Esther 5:7b-8).

Another banquet? Why didn't she just spit it out . . . why the cold feet?

Some commentators believe Esther simply choked. Staring at the king
and Haman—the two most powerful men in the country and the arbiters of
the soon-coming Jewish genocide—she just couldn't say it. Frankly, we can
understand why.

There's the king and Hitler sitting across the table. Demonically
inspired, terribly intimidating—he was the cold-blooded enemy of her people. Certainly she was terrified throughout the meal and probably struggled
to somehow appear happy and—well—normal.

Other scholars, however, assert that this is more of a manipulative ploy
on the part of Esther, since she had succeeded in getting the king to *agree* to
whatever it was that she wanted before he even *knew* what it was.

Wives have been doing that for centuries.

But the problem with this view is that Esther had *already* received affirmation from the king that she could have *anything* she wanted. She didn't
need another meal to nail it down.

If anything, she ran the risk of provoking his irritation by delaying her
request another day.

Regardless of *why* Esther decided not to speak at this seemingly opportune time, God's providence was the real reason for her delay.

It was God's plan that she wait to share her secret with the king. God was
about to direct circumstances in ways Esther could never have imagined . . . over
the course of one very sleepless night.

There were things taking place that were not only beyond Esther's power
but beyond her knowledge, as well.

She had no idea that the very next morning before he arrived for the second banquet, Haman was planning to kill Mordecai. If he succeeded in his evil
scheme, then Esther's decision to put off the request for one more night would
mean she wouldn't be able to save the one Jew she wanted to save the most.

But this is why the Book of Esther is not a revelation of how clever
people are—it's a dramatic demonstration of how clever God is. The story

is filled with people who continually try to plot and scheme their will into existence but, all along, God was weaving their schemes into His will of redemption.

Mordecai didn't know that he was less than twenty-four hours away from hanging on the gallows . . . but God knew. Esther didn't know her second banquet would be too late to save Mordecai's life . . . but God knew.

Before we underscore God's plans for deliverance, notice the fuel Mordecai piles onto Haman's fire of hatred and murder:

> *Then Haman went out that day glad and pleased of heart; but when Haman saw Mordecai in the king's gate and that he did not stand up or tremble before him, Haman was filled with anger against Mordecai* (Esther 5:9).

Evidently Mordecai knew that Esther had been welcomed by the king and he was no longer outside the administration building wearing sackcloth and ashes. He was back inside, behind his desk.

When Haman swaggered through the building on his way home after the banquet, Mordecai stayed seated while the others bowed before him. Mordecai effectively insulted the prime minister in front of all the servants and palace officials.

Well, that was the last straw.

But instead of immediately lashing out like his boss was known to do, Haman *controlled himself, however, went to his house, and sent for his friends and his wife Zeresh* (Esther 5:10). In other words, he wasn't about to let anybody spoil his party. He had some great news to share with his family and friends, and nothing—not even that old Jew refusing to bow to him—could rob him of his excitement.

NARCISSUS REINCARNATE

Just listen to him go on and on about himself:

> *Then Haman recounted to them the glory of his riches, and the number of his sons, and every instance where the king had magnified him and how he had promoted him above the princes and servants of the king* (Esther 5:11).

In ancient Hebrew, it reads, "Yada, yada, yada."

Haman was like the legendary Greek character Narcissus who loved his own reflection more than anything else. He was so enamoured of himself that he became the object of his own devotion. The world—his world—revolved around him.

Do you know anybody like that? Have you ever worked with someone like that?

- They get invited somewhere and you have to hear all about why they were chosen.
- They get a promotion and you have to hear every reason why they deserved it.
- They purchase something new and you have to look at it, admire it, tell them how much you wish you had the same thing, etc.
- They come back from a trip and everyone in the office has to endure the endless play-by-play . . . and a few dozen pictures.

There's a little song kids learned when I was a boy:

> *Oh, it's so hard to be humble*
> *When you're perfect in every way;*
> *I can't take my eyes off the mirror*
> *'Cause I get better lookin' each day.*

I learned it a long time ago at summer camp; it was obviously a spiritual highlight . . . that's all I can remember about camp.

I'm convinced this must have been Haman's favorite song and he sang it every chance he got. He made sure his servants, his family, and his friends sang it, too.

He brought together his wife Zeresh and the rest of his companions to tell them yet again why the king admired him so much, why Persia would not be the same without his leadership, how he'd been invited to dine with the king and queen, yada, yada, yada (that Hebrew word again!).

Haman was one big hot-air balloon. He was self-conceited, self-promoting, self-applauding, and self-absorbed.

Notice what else he said:

> **"Yet all of this does not satisfy me every time I see Mordecai the Jew sitting at the king's gate"** (Esther 5:13).

So here in the midst of his celebration he reveals that, deep down, he is still unhappy. This is classic human nature, isn't it?. I've got 99 things, but I want 100.

The one thing that lies beyond our reach often keeps us from enjoying the thousand things within our grasp.

If you hold two quarters in your hands and stretch your arms out in front of your face, you can see them easily enough, and everything else around them. But move the quarters right in front of your eyes and notice what happens to your vision: you can't see anything else.

Fifty cents can be all it takes to obscure our vision and keep us from seeing others.

Is there anything blocking your vision today? Are you gripping something so closely to your heart that it's keeping you from seeing anything—or anyone else?

The truth is we're a lot more like Haman than we want to admit. Our favorite person to please is ourself. Our favorite topic of conversation is who we are and how we feel and what we want. The person we think most deserving of love and admiration is our own self. *We* are our greatest roadblock to contentment.

Oh, that we would long for God to remove from our eyes those things that obscure our vision so that we may **regard one another as more important than [our]selves** (Philippians 2:3), so our Lord might become the greatest and dearest object of our devotion *(Psalm 73:25)*.

Haman's craving for *one more thing* would be his undoing . . . it could be ours, as well.

After pouring out both his joys and struggles to his wife and friends, they gave him unwise counsel:

> **"Have a gallows fifty cubits high made and in the morning ask the king to have Mordecai hanged on it; then go joyfully with the king to the banquet." And the advice pleased Haman, so he had the gallows made** (Esther 5:14).

Keep in mind that Esther didn't know anything about this; Mordecai didn't either. He was to be arrested the following morning and hanged on the gallows before lunch, regardless of what happened at Esther's next dinner party.

To the Persians, a gallows referred to being impaled on a sharpened pole and publically displayed.[3] There would be a raised platform or hillside which would support the pole so everyone could see the disgraced victim.

Zeresh told her husband Haman to make sure it was at least 75 feet high. In other words, "Make sure everyone can see Mordecai hanging, so everyone knows your power over life and death; make certain that everyone knows that to refuse to bow before you will bring them to their end."

What advice.

Frankly, this is the lowest point in the drama. This is where God seems to have completely abandoned His people. Things have never looked worse. Mordecai was a dead man . . . God had to do something that very night. And that is exactly what happened.

INSPIRED INSOMNIA

Our next scene opens with an irreversible case of divinely ordered insomnia:

> *During that night the king could not sleep so he gave an order to bring the book of records, the chronicles, and they were read before the king* (Esther 6:1).

I love this scene. There was the king in his bedroom that night, and he simply could not fall asleep. He had read the newspaper; he tried counting sheep; he thumbed through *Better Homes and Gardens* (that'll knock him out) . . . but nothing worked.

So he called a servant to come in and read to him from the annals of Persian history: literally the "words of the days."[4] This was the Persian equivalent of the Congressional Record—which would surely put anyone to sleep.

The Persians were world-renowned for their administrative care in record keeping, so you can imagine how long those scrolls were.

But somehow, of all the records the servant could have unrolled, it was the detailed account of the conspiracy against King Ahasuerus and how Mordecai had rescued him, just in time.

The reading of this five-year-old event accomplished two very important things: it reminded the king of Esther's loyalty to him, and it also brought up the name of Mordecai in a very positive, courageous light. But it revealed something that was somewhat embarrassing. The king asked the servant:

> *"What honor or dignity has been bestowed on Mordecai for this?" Then the king's servants who attended him said, "Nothing has been done for him"* (Esther 6:3).

This was entirely out of character with Persian customs. Ahasuerus' father and grandfather had rewarded faithful citizens with jewelry and garments. His great-great grandfather Cyrus had even given a loyal general a horse with a solid gold bridle and a dagger, along with a beautiful Persian robe.[5] Those loyal recipients were even given a special title in the kingdom—they were the "King's Benefactors."[6]

Ahasuerus, like his forebears, rewarded noble servants as well. He had already gifted faithful admirals with plots of land, and he had made one man the Governor of Cilicia as a reward for saving his brother's life. So by his own high standards of governance, failing to reward Mordecai for his service was an exceptional blunder.

The king immediately realized all of that. But he also knew that Mordecai was a Jew, which put him in an even greater predicament. How could he promote someone he had already condemned to death?

Ahasuerus had either completely overlooked the connection between Mordecai's lineage and the edict which he'd signed a few weeks earlier or, more than likely, Haman never actually identified the people he wanted to see wiped off the face of the earth.[7]

In fact, when you scour *Esther 3* for clues as to what the edict said and why the king signed it, you discover that Haman had actually written it *himself* and signed it with the king's seal.

In Ahasuerus' disregard for human life, he never cared to find out who Haman was seeking to destroy. There's actually no mention between Haman and the king that the people to be eliminated are *Jews*.

So, just about the time the servant informed the restless king of these matters, guess who showed up at the king's court?

Haman.

He had just finished building the gallows and was simply too excited to sleep. So he decided to go to work early in anticipation of his "best day ever."

He was about to be rid of the one man left in the nation who refused to venerate him, and he also had another dinner reservation with the king and queen.

Haman's hot-air balloon was sailing higher than cloud nine.

The king saw him and asked:

*"**What is to be done for the man whom the king desires to honor?**"* (Esther 6:6*a*).

Obviously Haman thought the king was speaking about him. So he responded with these words:

> *"For the man whom the king desires to honor, let them bring a royal robe which the king has worn, and the horse on which the king has ridden, and on whose head a royal crown has been placed"* (Esther 6:7-8).

How did Haman come up with this list so quickly? He'd already thought long and hard about how he'd like to be honored in public.

And it included wearing the king's robe, his crown, and riding his horse, too.

That's like the president of the United States offering you a free plane ticket but then allowing you, instead, to take your trip on Air Force One.[8]

As the prime minister, Haman had enjoyed everything but the throne. He had plenty of money, power, and prestige, but he wasn't king. So he didn't just want to be treated well *by* the king for the afternoon . . . he wanted to be treated *like* the king. That was why he wanted to wear the king's own robe.

Anybody can buy a copy of their favorite player's jersey from a ballpark vendor, a sporting goods store, or an online store, but to have one that *belonged* to a major league player—one that he actually wore during a game—now, that's entirely different.

And that's exactly what Haman wanted.

It helps to understand that in the ancient Middle East, your garments were considered a part of your being. What you wore actually represented who you were. Consider some examples of this:

- Aaron's priestly garments were given to his son to wear when he inherited the priestly office *(Numbers 20)*.

- Elisha received Elijah's mantle/cloak, which represented the designation of prophet *(2 Kings 2)*.

- The army commanders spread their clothes on the stairs for Jehu to walk on, which signified he had authority over their lives *(2 Kings 9)*.

- Luke's Gospel tells us that when Jesus rode into Jerusalem on a donkey, the people spread out their garments on the road for Him to ride over, symbolically submitting their lives to Jesus *(Luke 19)*.

As far as Haman was concerned, this was truly turning out to be the best day of his life!

THE GREAT REVERSAL

What happened next turned Haman's dreams to ashes:

Then the king said to Haman, "Take quickly the robes and the horse as you have said, and do so for Mordecai the Jew, who is sitting at the king's gate; do not fall short in anything of all that you have said" (Esther 6:10).

"What?. Are you kidding me? Mordecai . . . the *Jew*?" Haman's jaw dropped open in unimaginable shock.

The Hebrew construction of this passage indicates that Haman himself would dress Mordecai in the king's robe and place him on the king's horse and then lead that horse through the city square, declaring why Mordecai was being honored.

Mordecai would go from mourning to ecstasy, while Haman would go from ecstasy to mourning.

This was a pivotal point in both of these men's lives, and it was a decisive moment in this great drama.

For Haman, it was a crushing blow. He quickly returned home to change clothes and get ready for dinner back at the palace. His demeanor had completely changed. His countenance had fallen. His wife and friends regathered and, instead of binding up his wounds, they gave him this ominous warning:

"If Mordecai, before whom you have begun to fall, is of Jewish origin, you will not overcome him, but will surely fall before him" (Esther 6:13).

They barely got those words out of their mouths before the king's chariot pulled up and Haman was whisked away to the second banquet.

Only God could have arranged the timing of these events. When considering this story as a chessboard and God as the Mover of the pieces, a friend once made this profound statement: "God can move a king as easily as He can move a pawn, and He can move a queen as easily as He can move a bishop. The game belongs to Him."

God was moving the pieces of this story with divine precision. He doesn't make a mistake. Every move precisely anticipates the next.

Consider all the moves we have seen so far:

- a queen who risked her life to invite the king to a banquet;
- a prime minister who determined to use a hanging to enhance his power;
- a queen who delayed in making her petition until a second banquet;
- a king who was plagued with insomnia;
- a servant who picked up just the right scroll to read to the sleepless king;
- a hero who saved the king's life but wasn't rewarded until the day he was unknowingly going to be executed;
- a killer at the top of the food chain who was forced to honor and reward his mortal enemy—the man he had intended to hang instead.

And to think that all of this came together in the course of twelve hours . . . during just one sleepless night.

Only God could do that. What an incredible picture of His wisdom and providence. In fact, this passage teaches us at least three unforgettable truths about His providence.

1. God is at work even when circumstances are uncontrollable.

I have little doubt that during that sleepless night, news was delivered to Mordecai and, perhaps, even to Esther about a gallows being constructed by Haman . . . maybe they even figured out for whom it was intended.

It's quite possible that this news galvanized Esther to deliver the stunning news of Haman's treachery to the king the very next evening; there would be no more delays.

All of this was God's perfect timing. God had wanted Mordecai's name brought before the king in a favorable manner—he had saved the king's life.—which prepared the king's heart to not only desire to save Esther's life, but her uncle's life, as well.

2. God is at work even when life is unpredictable.

Can you imagine the roller coaster Mordecai had been on for the past five years? Think about it:

- he was a nobody from nowhere;
- he was promoted to work directly for the king inside the administrative wing of the palace, thanks to Esther's crown;
- he was sentenced to death, along with all the Jews, by Haman's irreversible edict;
- he lamented in sackcloth and ashes and turned back to his long-forgotten God;
- he saw the shadow of a gallows being built for him and had no recourse;
- he was not hanged but was rewarded by the king and dressed in his royal robes.

Mordecai should have had motion sickness by now.

Count on it: life will always be unpredictable, but God is at work, even still.

The lesson to be learned here is that stability in life never comes from *life*—it comes from trust in the One who gave us life.

3. God is at work even when sin seems unstoppable.

The edict had been written. It was the Law of the Medes and Persians—which means that it was unchangeable. The nearby gallows was seven stories high. A murderer was in control of the kingdom. A callous dictator was on the throne. Sin reigned while sanity had evidently been exiled.

But the Psalmist noted, ***He who keeps Israel will neither slumber nor sleep*** (Psalm 121:4), which is another way of saying, "God never goes off duty."

So when you have trouble sleeping, He's awake with you. And when you finally drift off to sleep, He doesn't.

Because God is never tired, *you* can be. Because God never sleeps, *you* can. You don't have to be in control of situations or circumstances or people, because God already is.

Even when the sun has disappeared and only the stars are visible, His angelic messengers are whirring about the universe doing His bidding. The events of life are His horsemen riding upon the winds of His will. *His* actions and counteractions, *His* plans and counterplans, are moving with perfect precision and perfecting power.

John Newton, the author of the famous hymn *Amazing Grace*, discipled a young man named William Cowper. But this close relationship didn't keep Cowper from struggling with bouts of suicidal depression.

One evening in 1774, Cowper called for a carriage and ordered the driver to take him three miles away to the Ouse River in England, where he planned to throw himself from a bridge.

The driver, discerning Cowper's suicidal intention, breathed a prayer of thanks when a thick fog suddenly moved in and enveloped the area. He purposely lost his way in the dense fog, driving up one road and down another, while Cowper fell into a deep sleep.

Several hours passed before the driver returned to Cowper's house. Cowper woke up and said, "How is it that we're home?" The driver answered, "We got lost in the fog, sir . . . I'm sorry about that." Cowper paid his fare, went inside, and pondered how he had been spared from harming himself by the clear providence of God.

There, that night in the solitude of his home, William wrote what would become one of his most famous hymns for the Church:

> *God moves in a mysterious way,*
> *His wonders to perform;*
> *He plants His footsteps in the sea,*
> *And rides upon the storm.*
>
> *Deep in unfathomable mines*
> *Of never-failing skill,*
> *He treasures up His bright designs*
> *And works His sovereign will.*
>
> *Judge not the Lord by feeble sense,*
> *But trust Him for His grace;*
> *Behind a frowning Providence*
> *He hides a smiling face.*[9]

Now the king and Haman came to drink wine with Esther the queen. ²And the king said to Esther on the second day also as they drank their wine at the banquet, "What is your petition, Queen Esther? It shall be granted you. And what is your request? Even to half of the kingdom it shall be done." ³Then Queen Esther answered and said, "If I have found favor in your sight, O king, and if it please the king, let my life be given me as my petition, and my people as my request; ⁴for we have been sold, I and my people, to be destroyed, to be killed and to be annihilated. Now if we had only been sold as slaves, men and women, I would have remained silent, for the trouble would not be commensurate with the annoyance to the king." ⁵Then King Ahasuerus asked Queen Esther, "Who is he, and where is he, who would presume to do thus?" ⁶And Esther said, "A foe and an enemy, is this wicked Haman." Then Haman became terrified before the king and queen. ⁷And the king arose in his anger from drinking wine and went into the palace garden; but Haman stayed to beg for his life from Queen Esther, for he saw that harm had been determined against him by the king. ⁸Now when the king returned from the palace garden into the place where they were drinking wine, Haman was falling on the couch where Esther was. Then the king said, "Will he even assault the queen with me in the house?" As the word went out of the king's mouth, they covered Haman's face. ⁹Then Harbonah, one of the eunuchs who were before the king said, "Behold indeed, the gallows standing at Haman's house fifty cubits high, which Haman made for Mordecai who spoke good on behalf of the king." And the king said, "Hang him on it." ¹⁰So they hanged Haman on the gallows which he had prepared for Mordecai, and the king's anger subsided.

–Esther 7:1-10

CHESS, CHECKERS, AND THE GAME OF LIFE

Esther 7:1-10

HANDICAPPING THE GAME

We have a little family tradition that started back when my kids were young, and we've managed to keep it to this day. Whenever we travel we stop for dinner at Cracker Barrel. The food's great, but the clincher is that they know how to make sweet tea like it was meant to be . . . sweet—the kind that can double for syrup if you're running low.

On many occasions while waiting for our table, I watched my kids arguing as they sat in those oversized rocking chairs, waging war over a game of checkers. The competition was always hot and heavy.

I have some fond memories of playing checkers against my kids . . . teaching them the valuable lesson of how to taste defeat with a good attitude. All except Charity, that is. She is our youngest, and I would sometimes let her beat me.

On one occasion, after beating my three older kids in checkers, they watched in horror as I lost to their six-year-old, blonde-headed, blue-eyed sister. Our twin sons quickly saw the injustice of this: not only was their little sister beating me, but they knew I was letting her. I explained to them later that whenever you play against a cute blue-eyed blonde, losing is a wise thing to do. I'm not sure they ever got the gist of my advice.

I also remember the moment when one of my sons nearly beat me. It was too close for comfort; in fact, he had me to the point where I actually thought to myself, *I'm finally going to lose to one of my kids and it won't be on purpose.* So I battled back.

At one strategic moment he forced me to jump him with one of my crowned pieces—a jump he had intended to use to trap me. But then I realized I could jump *backwards* over one of his other men, avoiding the trap altogether. The victory was soon mine.

My son wanted an immediate rematch, but our food had arrived and there was just nothing I could do about it. All the way to the table he kept saying, "I almost beat you . . . I would have beat you if you hadn't gotten that double jump."

I thank God for that double jump.

My father taught me a similar lesson through ping-pong when I was growing up. My parents had started a ministry for military men and women stationed in Norfolk, Virginia, and for years operated a thriving center for them in the middle of downtown. Sailors docked nearby would come to the center and play ping-pong, chess, checkers, eat snacks, and ultimately hear the Gospel of Christ. It was a wonderful ministry that I was grateful to be part of during my childhood.

I still remember watching cocky sailors come into the center and challenge my dad to a game of ping-pong. They had no idea what they were up against. He would stun them by pulling up a chair at the other end of the table and sitting down. His opponent would laugh and say, "You don't think you can beat me sitting down, do you?." My father would smile and say something like, "Well, let's see." Then, to my youthful delight, he would completely demolish them. He would then use their defeat to provide an introduction to the Gospel. After their humiliating trouncing, he would often say something like this:

See, young man, you came in here full of confidence in your own ability, only to discover that you weren't good enough to beat me. One day you will stand before God full of confidence in your own goodness, only to discover you aren't good enough to get into His kingdom.

Many young servicemen accepted Christ because of my father's simple strategy.

My grandmother used a tactic akin to my dad's. My three brothers and I called her Granny, and she was a tender-hearted woman, always smiling and kind to strangers. But put a chessboard in front of her and she became a completely different person altogether. She still wore the smile of a senior *saint*, but beneath that exterior was a ruthless competitor.

It wasn't long before a game of chess with her became a game of *chase*. I would move my king all over the board, trying to dodge all her pieces which were still in play. The end was inevitable. I merely waited for the moment when her blue eyes would look at me over her spectacles and her little voice would whisper that dreaded word, "Check." And a few moments later, "Checkmate."

Those games are so much like life, aren't they?

Just about the time you think you've got a plan mapped out for the next few moves, life suddenly delivers that shocking little word, "Check." It stuns you at first. Where? How? You didn't see it coming.

And it's not long before the game of chess becomes a game of chase.

One of the key lessons my grandmother taught us about chess—and I still remember it to this day because she repeated it often—was to *keep your eye on the queen*. The queen was to be protected and guarded as much as the king. The queen was the most powerful offensive piece on the board. We were instructed never to ignore the movement of our opponent's queen. "That's the key," she would say, "and never forget where the queen is located at all times."

Haman could have taken a lesson from my little granny. The cause of his downfall was exactly that: he failed to keep his eye on the queen. He had overlooked her . . . underestimated her . . . failed to consider her importance in the match. And that would be his undoing.

WHERE'S THE QUEEN?

Haman had just finished building a 75-foot gallows upon which to hang his unyielding colleague, Mordecai—a death that he intended as a grave foreshadowing of the fate of every Jew in Persia.

He had already mapped out the next few moves with deadly precision. He had Mordecai in "check" and was now only hours away from declaring a cruel but decisive "checkmate."

But then something unexpected happened.

All of a sudden, in a series of events, the tables were turned.

Haman hadn't done his homework. He had been knocking piece after piece off his opponent's board without noticing the most important one: the queen. He had failed to keep his eye on the queen.

Chapter 6 ended with Haman leaving for Esther's second dinner party after being warned by his family that his career was in jeopardy.

Unknown to him, there was more than a career to lose:

> ***Now the king and Haman came to drink wine with Esther the queen. And the king said to Esther on the second day also as they drank their wine at the banquet, "What is your petition, Queen Esther? It shall be granted you. And what is your request? Even to half of the kingdom it shall be done"*** (Esther 7:1-2).

The king hadn't forgotten the main reason for these banquets, and he was dying to know what Esther wanted.

> ***Then Queen Esther answered and said, "If I have found favor in your sight, O king, and it please the king, let my life be given me as my petition and my people as my request; for we have been sold, I and my people, to be destroyed, to be killed and to be anni-hilated"*** (Esther 7:3-4*a*).

Not only does Esther finally let the cat out of the bag, she actually *quoted* directly from Haman's edict: we are going to be **destroyed, killed and anni-hilated** (Esther 3:13).

No longer a jellyfish. The intimidation factor is gone. If she had been silent, she could have kept all her trinkets, cosmetics, attendants, and prop-erty. That meant nothing to her now.

All she wanted was life—for herself and for her people.[1]

Keep in mind that for a little more than five years she had kept her secret safe from the king. Her motto had been, "I'm a Jew on the inside but a Persian on the outside."

It's quite possible that she could have tried to maintain her secret and simply tell the king, "Listen, some of my best servants are Jewish and I like Jewish people, so I don't think it's very nice of Haman to try to kill them."

Instead, twice in this courageous petition, Esther openly declared to the king and his Jew-hating friend just who she was—Who she belonged to, both in life and in death. "I am a Jew, Ahasuerus . . . and if they perish, I perish with them."

The king wasn't quite catching on yet, but Haman was. His game of chess had just turned into a game of chase.

Esther created even more suspense:

"Now if we had only been sold as slaves, men and women, I would have remained silent, for the trouble would not be commensurate with the annoyance to the king" (Esther 7:4b).

That was a fascinating admission by Esther. She told the king that if the Jewish people were merely being sold into slavery, she wouldn't have said anything to him. But they weren't being sold . . . they were to be slain.[2]

This was altogether stunning news to both men. The king was hearing that his wife was in danger, and he probably didn't even know why. Esther wisely avoided giving any details that would implicate the king; after all, it was his signature on the death warrant.

As stated in the last chapter, Ahasuerus most likely allowed Haman to write the edict without ever being informed about the particulars of the coming massacre. All he knew was that traitors were going to be put to death and more money would flow into his coffers. What could be better than that?

It wasn't until later that Esther told the king the whole story, including the fact that she and Mordecai were cousins. For now she simply wanted her husband to know that someone out there planned to kill her and her extended Jewish family. Her timing was perfect . . . and her cunning was remarkable.

Haman, however, had *just* discovered, to his great shock, that Esther was a Jewess. Unlike the king, he understood her message loud and clear. He wrote the edict that she just quoted from, and he knew this information didn't bode well for him.

Esther's strong language, "**destroyed, killed and annihilated**," was taken directly from the portion of his edict that left no loophole for the life of any Jew. He had been anxiously awaiting the day when he could lawfully take off their heads, ending their bloodline and vindicating his forefather King Agag.

But now, to his horror, he found that Queen Esther was one of *them*.

He hadn't kept his eye on the queen, and I'll bet he was scratching his head at that moment, trying to figure out how he had missed that. He was sickened by the thought of what must come next. He had to make a move, and fast. The king was enraged. The only thing Ahasuerus heard was that someone was after his beloved wife and her family—which meant that someone was also trying to undermine his throne.

But who could it possibly be?

Now watch as the queen makes her final move:

> *Then King Ahasuerus asked Queen Esther, "Who is he, and where is he, who would presume to do thus?" And Esther said, "A foe and an enemy, is this wicked Haman."* (Esther 7:5).

Checkmate!

This normally meek queen hurled a dagger with that statement. Did you notice that she didn't just blurt out Haman's name. She actually raised the tension of the moment even more by describing the man as a wicked foe and an enemy to the king himself. And only then she stated the name of the traitor: Haman.

GAME OVER!

> *Then Haman became terrified before the king and queen* (Esther 7:6*b*).

He must have been trembling . . . his face deathly pale. All of the walls he had carefully constructed were crashing down around him. He couldn't possibly think what to do next.

The king was so shocked and infuriated that all he could do was get up and rush into the garden to digest what had just happened:

> *And the king arose in his anger from drinking wine and went into the palace garden* (Esther 7:7*a*).

And what must Ahasuerus have thought? He had quite a situation on his hands. In fact, he was feeling the corners of the chess board himself—his world had begun to look a little like *chase*:

- How could he punish Haman for an edict stamped with his own royal seal?

- How could he deal with Haman without admitting his own role?

- How could he rescind the decree which was now the Law of the Medes and Persians?

- How could he possibly soften the law that demanded the total destruction of all Jews when it left no loophole?

- How could he somehow protect Esther's life, while at the same time protect his own reputation?

- And if he couldn't . . . how was he going to explain her death?

The king was probably infuriated with himself, as he wondered:

- Why did I trust Haman so completely?

- Why in the world did I sign that edict?

- And why didn't I read the fine print?.

One author summarized it this way:

Who knows how many edicts Ahasuerus had signed on that day? Who knows how many pressing matters of government had been on his mind? He had countless decisions to make. And Haman, who was a trusted official, had proposed it in such a way that he seemed to be solving a problem that directly affected the good of the kingdom."[3]

While the king pondered all of those things alone in his garden, Haman made one final, desperate move:

Haman stayed to beg for his life from Queen Esther (Esther 7:7*b*).

Haman made a split-second decision there. He obviously decided that joining the king in the garden would be a bad move. He could tell by the expression on the king's face that he was in deep trouble. He also decided against running away, which would only confirm guilt, not to mention the fact he wouldn't get very far.

Haman knew he had been *checked* on almost all sides now,[4] but what he still didn't know was why.

He hadn't figured out yet who he had been playing against. He had been pitting his wits against the Jews for so long that he failed to take into account the *God* of the Jews. Haman was in way over his head—the entire match, his opponent had actually been God.

God had moved the queen into position—a queen Haman should never have taken his eyes off of—and now all Haman could do was ask . . . *beg* . . . for mercy.

Don't miss the irony of this scene: Haman was begging for his life from someone he had already *condemned* to death.

In fact, Esther couldn't save him if she had wanted to. She couldn't even save herself. According to the edict, she had less than eleven months to live.

In essence, they were *both* begging for their lives at this banquet. And according to the Law of the Medes and Persians, even the king himself might not be able to save them. But one thing was sure: he couldn't save them *both*.

The text tells us that in his terror—and implied anger—**Haman was falling on the couch where Esther was** (Esther 7:8*a*), where she had reclined during dinner.

Persian law stated that no man was allowed within seven paces of any member of the king's harem. In fact, that law also held that touching the king's wife was punishable by death.[5]

In his frustration and terror, Haman actually fell on Esther's couch— more than likely knelt over her and perhaps even grabbed her by the shoulders.

I can imagine that this man's ego, as well as his utter hatred for the Jews, was spilling out all over this scene. His clenched hands and terror-stricken cries of desperation must have turned to irrational cries of fury as he reproached the queen: "Who do you think you are? I'm the prime minister of Persia and you're just a common Jewess. You're the one who ought to die. How dare you trap me like this."

But while he had her pinned to the couch in an evidently threatening posture, the king returned to the dining room. I imagine the blood rushed to his face at that moment, as he saw Haman hovering over his wife. Scripture gives us a glimpse of his state when he shouted with rage,

"Will he even assault the queen with me in the house?" (Esther 7:8*b*).

In other words, "Is he going to kill my wife right in front of me?"

As the word went out of the king's mouth, they covered Haman's face (Esther 7:8*c*).

According to Persian custom, a condemned man was no longer worthy to be looked upon or to look upon another. So Haman's face was covered at once, indicating he was condemned to die.

But how would the king move so quickly to execute Haman? The Greek historian Herodotus gives us a clue when he explains that Persian law required at least two serious accusations against a citizen before they could be convicted and put to death.

The king now had both: Haman's plot to kill the Jews—which could be shown to be a direct threat against his own wife—and Haman's assault on the queen.

But then, out of nowhere, certainly unexpected by Esther, a third offense was revealed:

Then Harbonah, one of the eunuchs who were before the king said, "Behold indeed, the gallows standing at Haman's house fifty cubits high, which Haman made for Mordecai who spoke good on behalf of the king." (Esther 7:9*a*).

Don't miss those last few words. This servant was making sure the king remembered who Mordecai was.

He suddenly spoke up, "Excuse me, your Highness, but you should take a look outside your window and see the gallows Haman built for Mordecai. You remember Mordecai, don't you? He's the hero you just made a benefactor because he saved your life. Evidently Haman wants to kill the man who spoke loyally on behalf of the king."

This tip from one of the servants tips the legal scales completely over.[6]

Because of this servant's testimony, everything was now viewed through the lens of political intrigue and the implication of disloyalty to the king. In fact, the Septuagint adds a verse to explain that Haman would be disgraced and executed for *treason*.[7]

Talk about a double jump . . . and a checkmate all at the same time.

THE GREAT STRATEGIST

God is the ultimate strategist . . . and the game belongs to Him. Even when He's silent, He is present. Even when He seems removed, He remains sovereign. Even when He seems to be running late, His purposes are fulfilled on schedule.

There are four observations of the way God moves the events of our lives—His chess pieces—into place, at just the right time.

1. **God often uses reversals in our lives to move us forward and make us wiser.**

Things were going so well for Esther and Mordecai at first. Esther had won the crown and Mordecai had been promoted to the king's personal administrative staff. Then, out of nowhere, disaster struck. An egomaniac named Haman got all bent out of shape because one Jewish staff member wouldn't grovel at his feet. So he decided to take his rage out on the entire Jewish population—hoping to settle an old score in the meantime.

But think about it. Had this edict never been signed and propagated throughout the Empire, Esther would have never revealed her secret.

She and Mordecai may very well have lived their entire lives in the comfort of the palace, refusing to identify themselves with the remnant of God.

It was the threat of impending death and the hopelessness from this decree that brought about their own personal revival. Fear and hopelessness brought them back to faith again and the reversal of their fortune took them back to the roots of who they really were.

God still uses reversals in our lives to bring us back to trust and dependence on Him.

2. God often uses unlikely things to carry out His thoughts.

Esther had no idea that one of the king's eunuchs would deliver the final piece of information that would seal the king's verdict.

What an unlikely source of support for the Jewish people. A eunuch who'd spent his life listening and serving suddenly spoke up and drove the final nail into Haman's coffin.

From the world's perspective he was just one eunuch among thousands—a pawn on the chessboard that no one paid much attention to. But God uses little people to accomplish great things.

God uses the weak and foolish things of the world to shame the wise.

Isn't it wonderful to see a pawn move forward to save the day?

3. God often puts us through great difficulty before providing deliverance.

If God wanted to simply deliver us from trials, He could do it quickly and painlessly. But He isn't as concerned with our deliverance as He is with our development.

If our Lord only wanted to make us comfortable, He wouldn't allow roadblocks and reversals and trials. His goal, however, is not to make us comfortable; His goal is that we *become conformed to the image of His Son* (Romans 8:29).

That's why He isn't as interested in delivering us *from* the challenges of life as He is in developing us *through* the challenges of life.

4. God offers a special partnership with those who submit to His providence.

This is the co-laboring principle that the Apostle Paul introduced to the Corinthian church:

Now he who plants and he who waters are one; but each will receive his own reward according to his own labor (1 Corinthians 3:8)

Paul isn't saying that some people have more important jobs than others; he's saying that we should serve wherever we're placed. We are all pieces in God's providential work, and each of us has an important part to play . . . an important move to make.

This was also Paul's encouragement to the believers in Philippi who supported him financially. He reminded them in **Philippians 1:22** and **4:17** that the fruit of his labor would abound to *their* account.

Ravi Zacharias tells a personal story in his book *Jesus Among Other Gods* that illustrates this point very well. While vacationing in India, he watched a father and son weave some of the most beautiful wedding saris he had ever seen. Here is his description of that process:

> The sari is, of course, the garment worn by Indian women. It is usually six yards long. Wedding saris are a work of art; they are rich in gold and silver threads, resplendent with an array of colors. The place I was visiting was known for making the best wedding saris in the world. I expected to see some elaborate system of machines and designs that would boggle the mind. Not so. Each sari was being made individually by this father and son team. The father sat above on a platform two-to-three feet higher than his son, surrounded by several spools of thread, some dark, some shining. The son did just one thing. At a nod from his father, he would move the shuttle from one side to the other side and back again. The father would gather some threads in his fingers, nod once more, and the boy would move the shuttle again. This would be repeated for days . . . for hundreds of hours . . . until you would begin to see a magnificent pattern emerging. The son had the easier task—just to move at his father's nod. All along, the father had the design in his mind and he brought the threads together. The more I reflect on my own life and study the lives of other believers, I am fascinated to see the design God has for each of us. It is His to design . . . it is ours to respond in obedience.[8]

Isn't that the message Esther's story teaches us, as well? Whether you are a servant in the queen's house or the queen herself, you are a co-laborer with God in His mission to both demonstrate and deliver His gracious Gospel.

So submit to His providence today—He's also the Master of the game of life. He has created not only *who* you are but the place *where* you are.

And it just so happens to be . . . for such a time as this.

On that day King Ahasuerus gave the house of Haman, the enemy of the Jews, to Queen Esther; and Mordecai came before the king, for Esther had disclosed what he was to her. ²And the king took off his signet ring which he had taken away from Haman, and gave it to Mordecai. And Esther set Mordecai over the house of Haman. ³Then Esther spoke again to the king, fell at his feet, wept, and implored him to avert the evil scheme of Haman the Agagite and his plot which he had devised against the Jews. ⁴And the king extended the golden scepter to Esther. So Esther arose and stood before the king. ⁵Then she said, "If it pleases the king and if I have found favor before him and the matter seems proper to the king and I am pleasing in his sight, let it be written to revoke the letters devised by Haman, the son of Hammedatha the Agagite, which he wrote to destroy the Jews who are in all the king's provinces. ⁶For how can I endure to see the calamity which shall befall my people, and how can I endure to see the destruction of my kindred?" ⁷So King Ahasuerus said to Queen Esther and to Mordecai the Jew, "Behold, I have given the house of Haman to Esther, and him they have hanged on the gallows because he had stretched out his hands against the Jews. ⁸Now you write to the Jews as you see fit, in the king's name, and seal it with the king's signet ring; for a decree which is written in the name of the king and sealed with the king's signet ring may not be revoked." ⁹So the king's scribes were called at that time in the third month (that is, the month Sivan), on the twenty-third day; and it was written according to all that Mordecai commanded to the Jews, the satraps, the governors, and the princes of the provinces which extended from India to Ethiopia, 127 provinces, to every province according to its script, and to every people according to their language, as well as to the Jews according to their script and their language. ¹⁰And he wrote in the name of King Ahasuerus, and sealed it with the king's signet ring, and sent letters by couriers on horses, riding on steeds sired by the royal stud. ¹¹In them the king granted the Jews who were in each and every city the right to assemble and to defend their lives, to destroy, to kill, and to annihilate the entire army of any people or province which might attack them, including children and women, and to plunder their spoil, ¹²on one day in all the provinces of King Ahasuerus, the thirteenth day of the twelfth month (that is, the month Adar). ¹³A copy of the edict to be issued as law in each and every province, was published to all the peoples, so that the Jews should be ready for this day to avenge themselves on their enemies. ¹⁴The couriers, hastened and impelled by the king's command, went out, riding on the royal steeds; and the decree was given out in Susa the capital. ¹⁵Then Mordecai went out from the presence of the king in royal robes of blue and white, with a large crown of gold and a

(Continued on next page)

(Continued)

garment of fine linen and purple; and the city of Susa shouted and rejoiced. ¹⁶*For the Jews there was light and gladness and joy and honor.* ¹⁷*And in each and every province, and in each and every city, wherever the king's commandment and his decree arrived, there was gladness and joy for the Jews, a feast and a holiday. And many among the peoples of the land became Jews, for the dread of the Jews had fallen on them.*   –Esther 8:1-17

Now in the twelfth month (that is, the month Adar), on the thirteenth day when the king's command and edict were about to be executed, on the day when the enemies of the Jews hoped to gain the mastery over them, it was turned to the contrary so that the Jews themselves gained the mastery over those who hated them. ²*The Jews assembled in their cities throughout all the provinces of King Ahasuerus to lay hands on those who sought their harm; and no one could stand before them, for the dread of them had fallen on all the peoples.* ³*Even all the princes of the provinces, the satraps, the governors, and those who were doing the king's business assisted the Jews, because the dread of Mordecai had fallen on them.* ⁴*Indeed, Mordecai was great in the king's house, and his fame spread throughout all the provinces; for the man Mordecai became greater and greater.* ⁵*Thus the Jews struck all their enemies with the sword, killing and destroying; and they did what they pleased to those who hated them.* ⁶*And in Susa the capital the Jews killed and destroyed five hundred men,* ⁷*and Parshandatha, Dalphon, Aspatha,* ⁸*Poratha, Adalia, Aridatha,* ⁹*Parmashta, Arisai, Aridai, and Vaizatha,* ¹⁰*the ten sons of Haman the son of Hammedatha, the Jews' enemy; but they did not lay their hands on the plunder.* ¹¹*On that day the number of those who were killed in Susa the capital was reported to the king.* ¹²*And the king said to Queen Esther, "The Jews have killed and destroyed five hundred men and the ten sons of Haman in Susa the capital. What then have they done in the rest of the king's provinces. Now what is your petition? It shall even be granted you. And what is your further request? It shall also be done."* ¹³*Then said Esther, "If it pleases the king, let tomorrow also be granted to the Jews who are in Susa to do according to the edict of today; and let Haman's ten sons be hanged on the gallows."* ¹⁴*So the king commanded that it should be done so; and an edict was issued in Susa, and Haman's ten sons were hanged.* ¹⁵*And the Jews who were in Susa assembled also on the fourteenth day of the month Adar and killed three hundred men in Susa, but they did not lay their hands on the plunder.* ¹⁶*Now the rest of the Jews who were in the king's provinces assembled, to defend their lives and rid themselves of their enemies, and kill 75,000 of those who hated them; but they did not lay their hands on the plunder.*   –Esther 9:1-16

CHAPTER EIGHT

THE ORIGINAL PONY EXPRESS

Esther 8:1-9:16

POSTING BY PONY

In 1860, three businessmen organized a mail service between St. Joseph, Missouri, and Sacramento, California. The business was launched with the rather unbelievable promise to deliver mail from Missouri to California in only ten days.

After the Gold Rush brought hundreds of thousands of Americans to the far west, getting the mail between the nation's coasts became an increasingly important problem. Nothing meant more to people who went west in the 1840s and 1850s than mail from home.

On April 3, 1860, the Pony Express began operations with the first rider leaving St. Joseph, Missouri, and the next day, the first eastbound run left Sacramento, California. The eastern mail was carried over 1,966 miles and delivered in Sacramento on April 13.

The Pony Express had 80 riders in use at any one time, traveling through seven states and using 400 horses, while 400 other employees functioned as station keepers, stock tenders, and route superintendents.

Demands on the riders were stringent: weigh less than 125 pounds; change horses every 10-15 miles; travel 75-100 miles at a stretch; average 10 miles per hour.

To be a Pony Express courier was to be engaged in one of the most dangerous jobs in the world, not only because of the endurance and horsemanship required to stay in the saddle but the need to outrun bandits and Indians. Riders were paid a salary of $100-$125 a month for risking their lives to carry the mail across the continent.

At 15 years of age, William ("Buffalo Bill") Cody was employed as a Pony Express rider; he made the longest non-stop ride from Red Buttes Station to Rocky Ridge Station, Wyoming, and back when he found that his relief rider had been killed. The distance of 322 miles over one of the most dangerous portions of the entire trail was completed in 21 hours and 40 minutes, using 21 horses. That's unbelievably good time on horseback.

In October 1861, crews strung the final telegraph lines cross-country and joined them in Salt Lake City, Utah, making the Pony Express obsolete. When the last mail run was completed in November 1861, only one delivery had been lost and 34,753 pieces of mail were sent across the continent by those colorful dispatch riders.

I found it interesting that the original Pony Express wasn't started by cowboys and businessmen in the 1800s but by the Ancient Persians.

The Greek historian Herodotus recorded that the Persian Empire was connected by postal stations every 14 miles.[1] In speaking of this ancient postal service, Herodotus marveled:

Nothing travels as fast as these Persian messengers. The entire plan is a Persian invention. Along the whole trail there are men stationed with horses and they will not be hindered from accomplishing at their best speed the distance which they have to travel.[2]

It was Herodotus' description of the Persian Pony Express that gave us the famous saying, "Neither snow, nor rain, nor heat, nor gloom of night stays these courageous couriers from the swift completion of their appointed rounds."[3] While the US Postal Service has no official motto, the popularly held belief is that it does, and that's because those words are chiseled in gray granite over the entrance to the New York City Post Office on 8th Avenue—the same words that came from Book 8, Paragraph 98, of *The Persian Wars* by Herodotus.[4]

While the American Pony Express served, primarily, the upper- and business-class, with each package costing $5 per half-ounce, the Persian Pony Express was used by everyone. In fact, the Persian government relied heavily on this nationwide service to communicate in a kingdom that stretched from modern-day Pakistan to North Africa.

And it was the Persian Pony Express which would deliver the mail from Haman announcing the sentence of death.

Every Jew would have seen the post, whether wealthy or poor. The word travelled as swiftly as the riders on their galloping horses, bringing news of unspeakable terror, grief, and despair.

The Jews were outnumbered and defenseless.

But the tables were suddenly turned when Esther risked her life to get the king's attention. Within twenty-four hours, Haman's plot was uncovered and he was hanging from his own gallows.

Most people stop reading the Book of Esther at this part of the story and think that her work was over—mission accomplished. Queen Esther could now sit back and enjoy the winter palace of Susa like never before.

Nothing could be further from the truth. Haman may have been dead, but his edict of death was still very much alive.[5]

The document had been sealed with the king's royal insignia; it was now the Law of the Medes and the Persians. So Esther's job was far from over. In fact, she was needed now more than ever.

PROMOTION

On that day King Ahasuerus gave the house of Haman, the enemy of the Jews, to Queen Esther; and Mordecai came before the king, for Esther had disclosed what he was to her. And the king took off his signet ring which he had taken away from Haman, and gave it to Mordecai. And Esther set Mordecai over the house of Haman (Esther 8:1-2).

Josephus informs us that in the late kingdom of Persia, treason and felony resulted in the forfeiture of property and wealth to the crown.[6] This forfeiture included houses, property, possessions, and even bank accounts.

When King Ahasuerus gave all Haman's property and possessions to Esther, we find that she gave it into the hands of Mordecai, who was suddenly the second most-wealthy person in the kingdom.

Just imagine, those two Jewish cousins occupied the two most powerful positions in the Persian Empire, other than the king himself.

And what a turn of events—the queen and the prime minister were *Jews*. This was God's hand at work in the glove of history.

It might look like a series of coincidences to us, but it was sovereign providence. This scene had been choreographed by the Creator.

Nevertheless, there was still a serious issue at hand. Even though Esther and Mordecai might have had reason to feel safe and secure, they were deeply concerned for their people.

PASSION

Then Esther spoke again to the king, fell at his feet, wept, and implored him to avert the evil scheme of Haman the Agagite and his plot which he had devised against the Jews. And the king extended the golden scepter to Esther. So Esther arose and stood before the king (Esther 8:3-4).

Some believe that this conversation between Esther and the king took place at a later time. I believe, however, that this is part of the same conversation where Mordecai had just been promoted.

Proof of this is found in **Esther 8:7**, where the king responded to both Esther and Mordecai *together*. The timing reveals something significant: instead of going out and celebrating their good fortune for a week or two, they were immediately interceding for the lives of the Jewish people.

Esther was once again risking the king's displeasure by asking him to grant another request. The heart of her request is found in this sentence, as she made the plea,

"Let it be written to revoke the letters devised by Haman" (Esther 8:5*b*).

But the king wasn't all that concerned. In fact, he basically responded in the next two verses with something I'll paraphrase to read, "Look, Esther, I've just given Haman's estate and position to your cousin; there's really nothing more I can do because, as you know, I signed the edict myself, and according to Persian law, it must stand. Tell you what . . . I'll let you and Mordecai write up a new document that seems good to you and I'll sign that one, too" *(Esther 8:7-8)*.

We know from history that the Persian kings prided themselves on their infallibility. Why would they ever need to repeal a law? Whatever they signed was always right. By revoking it, Ahasuerus would be admitting that he had made a mistake. And he wasn't in the business of admitting mistakes.

True to his character, he squirmed his way off the hook while, at the same time, pleasing his wife and his right-hand man. Ahasuerus had found a loophole just large enough to wriggle through, and in the process he also did something critically important for the Jews.

PERMISSION

The king said to Esther and Mordecai,

"Now you write to the Jews as you see fit, in the king's name, and seal it with the king's signet ring; for a decree which is written in the name of the king and sealed with the king's signet ring may not be revoked" (Esther 8:8).

In other words, the king wouldn't *admit* that his first edict was ill-advised, but he suggested something that would exonerate himself from any embarrassment that the first decree might cause him in the future: "Aha. I'll send this second edict out, which will override the first—without having to admit the first one was foolish. Brilliant."

Frankly, Esther and Mordecai weren't the only ones who needed an escape clause. Don't overlook the fact that while the king would be allowing Esther to save her people's skin, behind the mask of cordiality, he was also saving his own.

Mordecai drew up a new law and had it copied in all the different languages of the Persian Empire. The letter basically endowed the Jewish people with several legal rights:

In them [these letters] *the king granted the Jews who were in each and every city the right to assemble* [an army] *and to defend their lives, to destroy, to kill, and to annihilate the entire army of any people or province which might attack them, including children and women, and to plunder their spoil, on one day in all the provinces of King Ahasuerus, the thirteenth day of the twelfth month* (Esther 8:11-12).

Well, the Jews had just been given the *legal* right to raise an army and take up arms. In fact, they were actually given the right to plunder any Persian who died while attempting to kill them.

Mordecai deftly quoted Haman's original edict word for word. All the Jews in Persia, who by now had the first edict memorized, immediately caught the significance of the wording in this second one. Mordecai was counterbalancing everything Haman established in the first decree: everything the Persians were told they could do, the Jews could now do.

The law was signed, sealed, and committed, and we're told:

The couriers, hastened and impelled by the king's command, went out, riding on the royal steeds; and the decree was given out in Susa the capital (Esther 8:14).

The news was now galloping from Susa to Sudan.

Two months earlier, the Persian Pony Express had delivered an edict of death throughout the empire. Ever since that time the sound of hoofbeats probably sent a shudder down Jewish spines, as they feared what news might be delivered next from the palace.

But now a Pony Express rider raced into town, and another letter with the king's insignia clearly visible was nailed to a post. People gathered, and suddenly shouts of joy erupted: "Mother! Father! Come quickly. Read the news of our deliverance!"

I can't imagine the dancing and celebrating of the Jews in the streets throughout the kingdom. Their day of death had been turned into a day of deliverance. This was their first ray of hope in months.

The new edict also sent a message to the Persian people that things had changed dramatically. All they needed to do now was restrain themselves and no one would get hurt—they would just lay off killing the Jews. If they kept their greed and animosity in check, no one would die.

Another thing this new law did was warn the Persians that they were no longer allowed to kill and steal from unarmed Jews. There wouldn't be a picnic of plundering. They would be risking their own lives and the lives of their families if they did, because *now* the Jews could retaliate in self-defense and plunder at will.

It was plain and simple: Persian citizens were no longer under orders to attack and kill Jews, but if they still chose to do so, it might not end well for them.

What a brilliant counterbalance to an unchangeable edict. What a wonderful turn of events for the Jewish people.

Can you imagine what it must have been like to be a Jew during that time? When you read the first edict two months before, life screeched to a halt. You knew you had less than eleven months to live. Your greatest fear had come to pass.

You had been wearing sackcloth and ashes for the last two months but your mourning and praying hadn't seemed to pay off. You imagined with horror what the thirteenth day of Adar was going to be like for you and your family and you knew you couldn't do anything to prevent it.

Your Persian neighbors and coworkers had been given the command from the prime minister to wipe you off the face of the earth and take your homes, possessions, and wealth for themselves.

Tension had been mounting in your village or town. Suspicions were growing every day. No one dared make eye contact with you. No one sympathized with you, for fear of reprisal from the government.

People were murmuring and gossiping about you in the streets and on the campus. You heard the things they were saying. Things like, "They must have been a threat to our government all along. You can't trust 'em. You know, when you think about it, they're not even Persians—they're just foreigners from a land they've abandoned. They never really fit in with us or our religion. Frankly, we'll be better off without them. The king's edict makes perfect sense . . . and the more I think about it, I like that Jew's house and chariot more than mine."

This was Germany and Austria and Poland 75 years ago, in the prelude to a later holocaust.

Then out of nowhere, a royal stallion gallops into your village with yet another scroll from the palace.

You creep up to the tree where it's posted and read it, but you can't believe your eyes. The new prime minister is Mordecai *the Jew*. The rumors that he had been executed by Haman were false. He is alive . . . and well . . . and in charge.

Furthermore, you discover in the edict that the king is now equally on your side. Even his government officials have signed on to abide by the second law.

This was cause for celebration, which was exactly what the Jewish people did:

> **Then Mordecai went out from the presence of the king in royal robes of blue and white, with a large crown of gold and a garment of fine linen and purple** [these were the royal colors of the palace in Susa]**; and the city of Susa shouted and rejoiced. For the Jews there was light and gladness and joy and honor** (Esther 8:15-16).

We're even told that **many of the people of the land became Jews** (Esther 8:17*b*). The Persians literally aligned themselves in solidarity alongside the Jews.

Some commentators believe this to mean that many Persians began following God, as well—the way that Rahab, the Gentile who abandoned her people in Jericho, became a proselyte Jew centuries later; or Ruth, who left her pagan idolatry, married a Jewish man, and later became the grandmother of King David.

No wonder the city of Susa was celebrating that night. We're told that for the Jewish people **there was light** (Esther 8:16*a*). That word *light* can be translated *hope*, representing the reversal of darkness.[7]

Everything was now filled with **hope and gladness and joy and honor** (Esther 8:16*a*).

What an amazing reversal.

The celebration would go nationwide. The Persian Pony Express galloped at full speed across the Arabian Desert, along the banks of the Euphrates River, down into India, and over into Africa, bringing the good news to everyone.[8]

Once seen as messengers of darkness and death, they were now seen as messengers of light and life.

PROTECTION

The clouds haven't completely parted, though. The day of the intended massacre was dawning, and the Jews, although they could now defend themselves, were vastly outnumbered.

Napoleon once remarked that God was always on the side of the largest army.[9] If he was right, then the Jews didn't stand a chance. Edict or no edict, death would still be imminent for some . . . perhaps, for all.

An account of their Day of Infamy opened with these words:

> ***Now in the twelfth month (that is, the month Adar), on the thirteenth day, when the king's command and edict were about to be executed, on the day when the enemies of the Jews* hoped *to gain the mastery over them, it was turned to the contrary so that the Jews themselves gained the mastery over those who hated them*** (Esther 9:1).

That verb translated *hoped* is a rare verb that refers to someone waiting with great anticipation.[10] In other words, many Persians were still salivating, considering the Jews to be easy prey. *We'll have new homes, fields, cattle, and clothing before the sun sets*, they thought. But we learn that the Jews, in fact, took mastery over *them*, instead.

Napoleon was wrong, after all.

Fighting had indeed erupted throughout the Persian kingdom but, at the end of the day, there was not one Jewish casualty. There was a record of Persians being killed, however, and most notable of that number were Haman's ten sons *(Esther 9:6-10)*.

Who could have imagined such divine protection, while thousands of Persians lost their lives when they acted with murderous intention.

An immediate celebration should have begun the following day; however, Esther did something surprising. She went back to the king and begged him to give the Jews *one more day (Esther 9:13)* to defend themselves.

She had evidently discovered a plot in Susa, more than likely fomented by Persians loyal to the ten sons of Haman who were killed in battle. There were many well-connected Persians in and around the palace who weren't happy with all these "divine reversals".

While the Jews were celebrating their survival, the next day would bring surprising attacks around the palace grounds. The lives of Esther and Mordecai may very well have been in danger.

But Esther didn't stop with the request of one more day. She also asked the king to publically display the bodies of Haman's ten sons *(Esther 9:13)* to discourage any further fighting.

Here's what those two days of bloodshed were like:

Now the rest of the Jews who were in the king's provinces assembled, to defend their lives and rid themselves of their enemies, and kill 75,000 of those who hated them; but they did not lay their hands on the plunder (Esther 9:16).

Upon reading this you might think, as I initially did, that 75,000 Persians is a large number of casualties—fighting must have taken place all over the kingdom.

But documents from this time period reveal that the population of Persia was somewhere around 50 *million* people, which means that the number of Persians who actually took up arms against the Jews was relatively small. [11]

God had obviously turned the hearts of the Persian citizens *toward* the Jewish people. If He hadn't, the Jews would have been easily annihilated without much of a fight.

By the way, don't miss the phrase that Ezra has already repeated three times as he recounted these events; remember, the Jews had been given the legal right to not only fight back but also to plunder any Persian citizen they defeated. But three times Ezra informs us **that the Jews did not lay hands on their plunder** (Esther 9:10, 15, 16).[12]

This was their chance to strike back. They had suffered a year of mental torture and anguish; they had received death threats; they had been attacked by neighbors who now lay dead in and around their homes. To take their possessions wouldn't be stealing; it wouldn't be unlawful in any way. Yet the Jews left their enemies' homes, possessions, and families alone.

Have you ever been ripped off by someone? Have you ever been mistreated by management in your company? Have you ever signed a contract only to find out the guy lied to you?

What would you do if somehow you were able to get back at them without any legal ramifications? What would you do to your enemy if you were offered the chance for revenge?

I heard a humorous story about a guy who was bitten by a dog and rushed to the hospital. Time lapsed, as both man and dog were tested. The doctor came in with the grim news that the dog was rabid and the man would likely develop rabies. There was no response except for the man taking a pad of paper and writing feverishly. His doctor, thinking he was writing out his last will and testament, encouraged him by saying, "Listen, you're not going to die; there's a cure for rabies." The man said, "I know that. I'm just writing out a list of people I want to bite."

That's the way of the world, isn't it? Don't get mad . . . get even. Bite back. One of mankind's natural instincts is revenge. While you might not use a gun or a sword, perhaps you've used a phone call or an email.

The Enemy of your soul knows that you will remain a victim much longer *if* you retaliate. Bitterness and anger will only steal your joy—you'll never find satisfaction in the destruction of an enemy.

That's why Satan never fails to show up and whisper in your ear, "You've held back long enough; you've gone the second and the third mile; why not get them back?"[13]

But the Jews didn't listen to that temptation. I can't help but think how remarkable their selfless actions were in light of the fact that they didn't have the New Testament, as we now have.

They couldn't open their Bibles and read what the Apostle Paul said:

> *Never pay back evil for evil to anyone. Respect what is right in the sight of all men. If possible, so far as it depends on you, be at peace with all men. Never take your own revenge, beloved, but leave room for the wrath of God, for it is written, "Vengeance is Mine, I will repay," says the Lord. Do not be overcome by evil, but overcome evil with good* (Romans 12:17-19, 21).

What has the mailman delivered to your door recently?

- bad news

- false accusation

- unkind words

- misfortune

- gossip

- slander

Have you heard the whispering of the Enemy: "You didn't do anything wrong; you've taken it on the chin long enough; it's time for a little revenge"?

Learn from those Jewish survivors who had *every* reason to take revenge on their enemies but, instead, refused to do anything more than defend their lives.

And don't think for a second their Persian neighbors didn't notice. The God of Israel received great honor that day as His people lived out these words:

> *But you are a chosen race, a royal priesthood, a holy nation, a people for God's own possession, that you may proclaim the excellencies of Him who called you out of darkness into His marvelous light* (1 Peter 2:9).

What's so amazing about this story is not that the Jews gained mastery over their enemies, but that they gained mastery over *themselves*.[14]

A national, empire-wide celebration ensued, and the Jewish remnant marveled that they were alive. And their joy was deeper and richer because they chose to leave revenge to the hand of God. Their celebration would have been a lot shorter and far less sweet had they chosen to plunder their neighbors.

The lesson remains: our world doesn't understand this principle. Books are written and movies are made all the time which glorify revenge. To truly turn the other cheek after suffering injustice is a concept that blows their minds. But it also makes them look twice at the person who responds without retaliation. And in the end, God receives glory and the Gospel gains more credibility because of it.

How will you respond to the news that might be delivered to your doorstep today? It's on its way right now. Will you, like those Jews, remind the world that in every circumstance God is worthy of praise and honor . . . or will you act like a Persian?

We—the Church—are a royal priesthood and a holy nation. Let's make it our ambition to demonstrate our commitment to our Savior who has called us out of darkness into His wonderful light.

^{16}*Now the rest of the Jews who were in the king's provinces assembled, to defend their lives and rid themselves of their enemies, and kill 75,000 of those who hated them; but they did not lay their hands on the plunder.* ^{17}*This was done on the thirteenth day of the month Adar, and on the fourteenth day they rested and made it a day of feasting and rejoicing.* ^{18}*But the Jews who were in Susa assembled on the thirteenth and the fourteenth of the same month, and they rested on the fifteenth day and made it a day of feasting and rejoicing.* ^{19}*Therefore the Jews of the rural areas, who live in the rural towns, make the fourteenth day of the month Adar a holiday for rejoicing and feasting and sending portions of food to one another.* ^{20}*Then Mordecai recorded these events, and he sent letters to all the Jews who were in all the provinces of King Ahasuerus, both near and far,* ^{21}*obliging them to celebrate the fourteenth day of the month Adar, and the fifteenth day of the same month, annually,* ^{22}*because on those days the Jews rid themselves of their enemies, and it was a month which was turned for them from sorrow into*

(Continued on next page)

(Continued)

gladness and from mourning into a holiday; that they should make them days of feasting and rejoicing and sending portions of food to one another and gifts to the poor. [23]*Thus the Jews undertook what they had started to do, and what Mordecai had written to them.* [24]*For Haman the son of Hammedatha, the Agagite, the adversary of all the Jews, had schemed against the Jews to destroy them, and had cast Pur, that is the lot, to disturb them and destroy them.* [25]*But when it came to the king's attention, he commanded by letter that his wicked scheme which he had devised against the Jews, should return on his own head, and that he and his sons should be hanged on the gallows.* [26]*Therefore they called these days Purim after the name of Pur. And because of the instructions in this letter, both what they had seen in this regard and what had happened to them,* [27]*the Jews established and made a custom for themselves, and for their descendants, and for all those who allied themselves with them, so that they should not fail to celebrate these two days according to their regulation, and according to their appointed time annually.* [28]*So these days were to be remembered and celebrated throughout every generation, every family, every province, and every city; and these days of Purim were not to fail from among the Jews, or their memory fade from their descendants.* [29]*Then Queen Esther, daughter of Abihail, with Mordecai the Jew, wrote with full authority to confirm this second letter about Purim.* [30]*And he sent letters to all the Jews, to the 127 provinces of the kingdom of Ahasuerus, namely, words of peace and truth,* [31]*to establish these days of Purim at their appointed times, just as Mordecai the Jew and Queen Esther had established for them, and just as they had established for themselves and for their descendants with instructions for their times of fasting and their lamentations.* [32]*And the command of Esther established these customs for Purim, and it was written in the book.*

–Esther 9:16-32

Now King Ahasuerus laid a tribute on the land and on the coastlands of the sea. [2]*And all the accomplishments of his authority and strength, and the full account of the greatness of Mordecai, to which the king advanced him, are they not written in the Book of the Chronicles of the Kings of Media and Persia?* [3]*For Mordecai the Jew was second only to King Ahasuerus and great among the Jews, and in favor with the multitude of his kinsmen, one who sought the good of his people and one who spoke for the welfare of his whole nation.*

–Esther 10:1-3

CHAPTER NINE

THE GOSPEL ACCORDING TO ESTHER

Esther 9:16–10:3

THE JOYOUS RITE OF CELEBRATION

My wife and I took a trip to Kill Devil Hills at Kitty Hawk, North Carolina, to see where Orville and Wilbur Wright flew their homemade invention—what would become the world's first controlled, sustained flight in a heavier-than-air craft. To this day, a memorial stands on the spot where they first lifted off more than a century ago.

Sons of a protestant pastor, these brothers had figured out the concept of "wing warping"—a system of manipulating the edges of a plane's wings to allow the wind to elevate or lower the plane, turn or keep it straight. It was the critical piece in the puzzle that no one had yet figured out.

And their ingenuity paid off. On December 17, 1903, the Wright brothers tossed a coin to see who would pilot the plane. Orville won the toss and climbed aboard the aircraft he and his brother had built in their bicycle shop back home. The airplane coasted down the sand bar on a wooden rail and then rose into the air for twelve seconds, traveling 120 feet.

It was one small step for man (the Wright brothers) . . . one giant leap for mankind—and the possibility of air travel!

While we were in Kitty Hawk, I picked up a 500-page biography of Orville and Wilbur titled *The Bishop's Boys*, and it catalogs not only the absorbing story of how they invented the airplane, but it also gives interesting accounts of their family life.

One of the things I read that intrigued me was the fact that their father originally believed God had not created man to fly. He wasn't all that happy with his sons' fascination with airplanes. In fact, for several years he never even asked for the opportunity to fly with them.

But after six years of watching his sons' success grow into a world-wide phenomenon, he finally relented and asked for a ride in their airplane—at 86 years of age. The boys were actually a little nervous; they weren't too sure how he'd react to flying through the air.

Orville was at the rudder and they flew around an open field for nearly ten minutes. At one point in the flight, Orville's father leaned close to his ear and shouted above the roar of the engine the words his son would never forget: "Higher, Orville, higher!"[1]

So much for the bishop's reservations against flight.

Today, you can stand beneath a massive 60-foot monument at Kitty Hawk, where a memorial has been erected as a constant reminder of two preacher's kids who changed the world.

Memorials are a great idea, aren't they? I think it's appropriate to build monuments and designate special days/seasons to specifically remember people and events.

Our calendar is dotted with dates dedicated to remembering defining moments in our nation's history, and memorials honor war veterans, holocaust victims, and great presidents.

These monuments give our *past* due significance and ultimately provide better perspective on our *present*.

They remind us that some things are worth remembering.

The last few paragraphs in the scroll of Esther give us exactly that—a memorial to events worth celebrating.

The truth is, Esther and Mordecai weren't about to let their deliverance go unnoticed by future generations. And so they established a memorial that is so, well, *memorable* that today—2,500 years later— Jewish people are still celebrating the season.

It's called the Feast of Purim.

Esther 9:17 says that the feast began as a spontaneous celebration. As soon as the fighting was over and the Jews marveled that they were still alive, they immediately began to rejoice.

In the latter part of that verse, Ezra comments that the ***feasting and rejoicing*** broke out all over the kingdom.

The war was over. Their lives were spared. And there was only one thing they wanted to do: celebrate!

This reminds me of the celebration that spilled into the streets after news hit the airwaves that World War II had just ended. People all over the world danced and laughed and hugged each other as if they were long-lost friends. There were no strangers on that day. Everyone was united in their joy.

Perhaps you've seen that classic photograph taken in Times Square just after the news was delivered. In the midst of all the spontaneous celebration, a sailor grabbed a young nurse in his arms and planted a big kiss on her. You probably thought it was just a romantic kiss between two young lovebirds. Not quite. It was actually a kiss shared between two complete strangers. The war was over and everybody was happy.

And I can overlook what that sailor did for two reasons: first, because his mind was somewhat foggy due to the excitement and, secondly, because the young lady wasn't my daughter!

Only those who have actually lived through a war understand the euphoria that comes at the end of it.

Well, the battle had just ended in Persia, and I imagine there were a lot of Jews kissing and hugging in the streets.

But what began as a spontaneous celebration became a fixed holiday tradition:

> ***Then Mordecai recorded these events, and he sent letters to all the Jews who were in all the provinces of King Ahasuerus, both near and far, obliging them to celebrate the fourteenth day of the month Adar*** [March]***, and the fifteenth day of the same month, annually, because on those days the Jews rid themselves of their enemies, and it was a month which was turned for them from sorrow into gladness and from mourning into a holiday; that they should make them days of feasting and rejoicing and sending portions of food*** [or gifts] ***to one another and gifts to the poor*** (Esther 9:20-22).

The celebration lasted for two days: March 14 was designated for those living throughout the kingdom and March 15 was designated for those living in walled cities such as Jerusalem.² And the Jewish people have never forgotten to celebrate since that day.

It's interesting that during World War II the Nazis hated any mention of the Book of Esther. In fact, one historian recorded that if a Jew arrived at one of the concentration camps with the Book of Esther in his or her possession, that Jew was immediately put to death.³

The Nazis wanted no message of hope or deliverance whispered inside the barracks of the death camps. Still, many of the inmates of Auschwitz, Dachau, and Treblinka produced written copies of the Book of Esther from memory and then huddled together, reading them quietly to each other in secret during the Feast days of Purim.⁴

The memorial still gave them hope . . . even inside a camp that had marked them for death.

What a convicting thing it is to consider a concentration camp as a context for remembering God's provision and protection. What unwavering hope and trust the Jews displayed as they looked back at Esther's memorial and clung to their belief that God would preserve them still.

To the Church today, composed of both Jewish and Gentile believers who've placed their faith in Jesus Christ, this Book is far more than an ancient revival account or a feel-good underdog story. It's a wonderful analogy to the truths of the Gospel.

I call it *the Gospel according to Esther*. It offers encouraging reminders for all believers everywhere—whether in a church pew or in a prison camp.

THE COMMONER QUEEN OF PERSIA

The first analogy that I find to the Gospel in this Old Testament book is that Esther, a common girl, became a queen.

For the first time in Persian history, the king forsook centuries of political tradition and placed the crown on the head of a young woman who was a common peasant, an orphan, a foreigner, and a child of exiled Jews.

Is that great or what?

Consider this: we are the fallen sons of Adam and daughters of Eve, as C.S. Lewis so poetically described us. We are common sinners alienated from God. But then God allows us to be adopted as sons and daughters into

His royal family, where we're given full rights and privileges as though we were part of his biological family all along *(Ephesians 1:5)*.

And if that isn't enough, He will also crown us as His bride and let us reign with Him in His future eternal kingdom *(2 Timothy 2:12; Revelation 22:5)*.

I need to remind myself on Sunday mornings that I'm not preaching to commoners—I'm preaching to royalty. I'm not encouraging peasants to follow Christ—I'm expounding the Word to future kings and queens.

What happened to Esther will happen to all of us who believe in Jesus Christ.

From commoner to royalty . . . talk about a great reversal.

- You'll trade the common clothes of mortality for the royal robes of immortality.
- You'll trade the body of failure and imperfection for a glorified body that is sinless and perfected in holiness.
- You'll trade the sorrow and sadness of earth for the joy and pleasure of heaven.
- You'll trade the fear and uncertainty of speaking to an invisible God for the thrill and wonder of speaking to God . . . face-to-face.

How is this possible? Because the King of kings has chosen you, a commoner, to be His bride.

THE IRREVOCABLE EDICT OF DEATH

The second analogy we discover from this Gospel according to Esther is bound up in the edict of death.

Just as the king had published an irrevocable decree of death for all Jews, so humanity is also under an irrevocable edict of death.

The Bible reveals:

[I]*t is appointed for men once to die once and after this comes judgment* (Hebrews 9:27).

It's important to note that the Jewish people during Esther's time weren't condemned because of *what* they had done. They were condemned because of *who* they were.

They were Jews. It was as simple as that. That fact alone brought them under the death penalty in the kingdom of Persia.

They didn't have to commit heinous crimes or get caught in some blatant act of treachery to fall under judgment. They simply had to belong to the Jewish race.

It's the same for us today, isn't it? We are under the King's edict of death because we belong to the human race. The murderer and the moral man will experience the same condemnation. The rich and educated will stand under the same reproach as the poor and illiterate. Serial killers and social workers are both under the irrevocable edict of death.

Look at a graveyard and you'll see a silent testimony to the impartiality of this irreversible law. God has written these unchangeable words into the edict, according to the Law of God: *The wages of sin is death* (Romans 6:23*a*).

The paycheck for simply belonging to a fallen human race is death. And as far as I can tell, the death rate is one out of one.

But there is more to this analogy. Do you remember that under Haman's edict the Jews were not allowed to defend themselves? Well, in the same way, the edict of death that we as humans are under has no escape clause either. We are completely *defenseless* against the justice of God's edict. There is nothing we can do to avoid death.

Oliver Winchester and his wife Sarah once lived in New Haven, Connecticut. Oliver is known for inventing the Winchester rifle—the first true repeating rifle, used by the Union Army during the Civil War.

Upon the invention of his rifle, government and private contractors made him unbelievably wealthy. Life went better than they could have dreamed for about four years. Tragically, Sarah gave birth to a daughter named Annie who died only two weeks after her birth. Sarah was so shattered by the loss that she became a recluse and nearly lost her mind.

Several years later, Sarah's grief was only compounded when Oliver contracted tuberculosis and died. She became the heiress to his vast fortune, but no amount of money could alleviate her loneliness and sorrow. At a friend's suggestion, Sarah sought to contact her deceased husband through a spiritist—a necromancer.

During her séance, the medium informed Sarah that her husband was in the room with them. According to the medium, Oliver was delivering the message that the Winchester family was cursed because of his invention of the Winchester rifle. The spirits of those who were killed by his rifle were seeking vengeance.

The spiritist told Sarah that the only solution was to move to a remote location and build a house for these spirits. Supposedly, Oliver had also communicated that as long as Sarah continued to build the house, she would live. But if she ever stopped building on that property and home, she would die.

Sarah immediately sold her home in New Haven, moved west with her fortune, and bought a home that was already being constructed on 162 acres of land. She bought the entire estate and then threw away the building plans.

For the next thirty-six years her construction crew built and rebuilt, altering one section of the house after another. The sounds of hammers and saws could be heard day and night. Railway cars brought in supplies, and every morning Sarah met with the foreman to sketch out new rooms.

Much of it had no rhyme or reason; rooms were added to rooms, wings were added onto wings; flat areas were transformed into towers and peaks; staircases were built that led nowhere. Doors were hung that opened to nothing, and closets were built that opened onto blank walls. Hallways even doubled back upon themselves as the house became a vast, expensive maze, designed to both house and confuse the evil spirits that tormented her mind.

Sarah Winchester depleted her fortune by building the sprawling, confusing mansion. But then, on the night of September 4, 1922, after holding another séance, Sarah Winchester went up to her bedroom and, at the age of 83, died in her sleep.

Oliver had told her that as long as she continued building, she would remain alive. He was wrong.[5]

Of course, it wasn't Oliver, anyway. A demon—or a crafty medium—had delivered a message that would distract Sarah Winchester and eventually destroy her.

We, as humans, like Mrs. Winchester, busy ourselves with hammers and saws: playing, enterprising, entertaining, eating, marrying, parenting, educating, working, investing, and planning—and all the while we hope the noise of the construction site will drown out the echo of that inevitable edict.

One journal article recently admitted that the health industry isn't passionate about discovering ways to help us live a healthier life; instead, it's obsessed with trying to discover a way to avoid death.

But this is the King's irrevocable edict. There is no higher court to which we can appeal; there is no jury to convince; there is no judge to influence; there is no loophole to escape the law of irrevocable death.

And any message otherwise is either demonic or devious.

THE TIMELY INTERCESSION OF ESTHER

The third analogy we discover in this Gospel according to Esther is Esther's intercessory work on behalf of the Jewish people.

After three days of solitude, Esther suddenly appeared before the king without any introduction and asked him to rescue her people. She willingly risked her life to save theirs.

I discovered in my studies that many Jewish rabbis and scholars believe Esther's three days of solitude are connected mysteriously to Jonah's three days in the belly of the fish.

Jewish tradition has taught for centuries that the dead will come to life after three days from the start of the final judgment. They base this on a misinterpretation of this Scripture:

> *"He will revive us after two days; He will raise us up on the third day that we may live before Him"* (Hosea 6:2).[6]

Properly understood, this prophecy provides a wonderful picture of the coming death and resurrection of Christ. After three days in the grave, Jesus rose again and now stands before God the Father, interceding on our behalf. He didn't merely *risk* His life for our sake . . . He *gave* His life for us.

Martin Luther wrote these profound words about this parallel between Esther and Christ:

> On the third day after judgment transpired on the cross, Jesus Christ arose, guaranteeing safety to enter God's presence to all who reach out in faith to touch the scepter which is in the shape of a cross[7]

It's true, isn't it? The Father gladly receives the petition of the Son and welcomes all those who come through Him. Jesus, our Intercessor, says, *"[N]o one comes to the Father, but through Me"* (John 14:6*b*).

THE EVERLASTING EDICT OF LIFE

The next analogy we recognize in Esther's Gospel is the fact that a second edict had been delivered—an edict of life.

The writer of Hebrews said:

"He [Christ] *is able to save forever those who draw near to God through Him, since He always lives to make intercession for them"* (Hebrews 7:25).

Previously I quoted the first half of **Romans 6:23**, which says, **For the wages of sin is death**, but you may be aware that the verse doesn't actually end with those words. That was only the first edict. The second edict is found in the second half of that verse:

[B]*ut the free gift of God is eternal life in Jesus Christ our Lord* (Romans 6:23*b*).

This second edict begins with an important conjunction—**but**—which is a critical little word. In fact, what follows this little word makes all the difference in the world.

Whenever you're having an important conversation with someone, the conversation that comes after the word **but** is what really matters.

Your boss calls you in and says, "That was a great job, **but** . . ."

Your girlfriend says, "I really enjoy being with you, **but** . . ."

Your child's teacher calls and says, "We really enjoy having your son in our classroom, **but** . . ."

That little conjunction has a way of grabbing our attention like few other words do.

When I was in fourth grade, there was nothing I dreaded more than to hear my mother answer the telephone in the evening and say, "Well, hello, Mrs. Jolly."

Mrs. Jolly was my fourth grade teacher. And she was such a tattletale. I always knew what would follow a conversation between Mrs. Jolly and my mother . . . it would usually be an edict of death.

Maybe for you it was a client who called and said, "We've enjoyed doing business with you; you've always done a great job, **but** . . ."

Or the doctor's office called to leave the message, "Everything looks good, *but* . . ."

Regardless, whatever comes after that little conjunction matters a whole lot more than what comes before it.

The latter can nullify the former.

In this text, that little word becomes the hinge upon which all eternity hangs:

> *For the wages of sin is death, <u>but</u> the free gift of God is eternal life in Christ Jesus our Lord* (Romans 6:23).

But—isn't that the greatest little word? Death . . . *but* life. An irrevocable edict of judgment . . . *but* an opportunity to receive salvation.

Through the work of Jesus Christ's intercession on our behalf, the edict of death has been nullified by an edict of life.

Jesus Christ said,

> *"I am the resurrection and the life; he who believes in Me shall live, even if he dies"* (John 11:25).

In other words, none of us can avoid the edict of death, but all of us can, by faith in Jesus Christ our Messiah, accept the edict of life.

The second edict brings life . . . hope . . . peace.

In the last chapter of Esther, we're told that Mordecai is second only to the king himself, and he used that power to promote the good of his people and seek *the welfare of his whole nation* (Esther 10:3).

That phrase literally reads *he spoke shalom*, which means he spoke *peace*. What a great way to summarize the interceding work of both Esther and Mordecai on behalf of their people.

That word says it all: shalom . . . peace.

The only place you'll find real peace on this planet is in the heart of someone who has been redeemed by Christ and reconciled to God. It's not a state of never-ending ecstasy or a happy thrill every day you climb out of bed; it's the knowledge that the wrath of God no longer rests on you. You are no longer helpless and defenseless under the edict of death, but forgiven and saved by the edict of life.

Our seminary hymn at Shepherds Theological Seminary puts it this way:

Before the throne of God above
I have a strong, a perfect plea,
A great High Priest, whose Name is "Love,"
Who ever lives and pleads for me.

My name is graven on His hands,
My name is written on His heart;
I know that while in heav'n He stands
No tongue can bid me thence depart,
No tongue can bid me thence depart.

When Satan tempts me to despair,
And tells me of the guilt within,
Upward I look and see Him there
Who made an end to all my sin.

Because the sinless Savior died,
My sinful soul is counted free;
For God, the Just, is satisfied
To look on Him and pardon me,
To look on Him and pardon me.

One man told me recently that he worked in New York on Wall Street for many years. He and his wife were financially and professionally successful. His office looked out toward the World Trade Center.

He recounted what it was like to witness 9/11. Through the windows of his office suite, he had watched the airplanes crash into the towers and the massive skyscrapers collapse. He saw everything: the panic, the suicide victims, the wreckage. Frankly, it was too much for him.

When he finally made it out of the city and home to his wife, they immediately decided to sell everything and move. They eventually ended up in North Carolina, where they began to search for spiritual answers. They visited one church after another, but nothing seemed to help.

Finally, ten years into their search, they visited our church—which was just a few miles from their home. When they later introduced themselves to me, I asked the husband why he had decided to stay at Colonial. He gave me an answer I'll never forget. He said, "When I sat down in a morning service, I felt *peace*."

They listened to the messages intently for months. Finally, the Gospel found receptive soil in this man's heart and he prayed at the end of a worship service as I prayed from the pulpit—a simple prayer of repentance and faith. His wife came to meet me after a service a few weeks later and announced that she also was ready to accept the Gospel of Christ for herself, and we prayed together as she gave her life to Christ.

A listener to *Wisdom for the Heart* wrote a very personal message, telling us that she had planned to take her life. Though a believer, she had suffered years of financial and physical setbacks, including 22 major surgeries. Then, only recently, her precious mother had died, making this woman the only living member of her family. She decided, as she put it, to end her life.

She woke up on that fateful day and turned on the radio for the last time. *Wisdom for the Heart* was on the air and as she listened, God used the message from His Word to change her mind about committing suicide. In her own words, that message caused her to surrender her will to God . . . no matter what.

The Gospel message not only redeems lives . . . it encourages and sustains life.

The Gospel provides not only peace *from* the guilt of sin, but peace *in* the midst of life's storms.

THE ENDURING REMINDER OF DELIVERANCE

The final analogy we can draw from this Gospel according to Esther is from the memorial Esther and Mordecai established nearly 3,000 years ago:

> *Therefore they called these days Purim after the name of Pur. And because of the instructions in this letter, both what they had seen in this regard and what had happened to them, the Jews established and made a custom for themselves, and for their descendants, and for all those who allied themselves with them, so that they would not fail to celebrate these two days according to their regulation, and according to their appointed time annually. So these days were to be remembered and celebrated throughout*

every generation, every family, every province, and every city; and these days of Purim were not to fail from among the Jews, or their memory fade from their descendants (Esther 9:26-28).

In other words, "Let's make sure we never *forget* this day. Let's build a monument; let's make a memorial to the providence of God in our deliverance . . . let's call it *Purim.*

The name *Purim* comes from the plural form of *Pur*—an Akkadian word for *lots.* Lots were small stones that were thrown from the hand like the rolling of dice. It's interesting that the English word still carries the same meaning today. We have a gambling game called "the lottery" and we often refer to our "lot in life."[8]

King David used this same word when he wrote,

"The LORD is the portion of my inheritance and my cup; Thou dost support my lot (Psalm 16:5).

In other words, David recognized that his lot in life was directly related to the providential work of God. He's the One who controls even the roll of the dice . . . there is no such thing as chance.

The Jewish people understood this as well, so it's no surprise that *Purim* was a time of great joy. In fact, the Jewish people still gather to this day to hear the reading of the Book of Esther and celebrate *Purim.* When their reader arrives at **Chapter 3** in the story, pandemonium erupts at each mention of Haman's name. Every time Haman's name is read thereafter, the audience delights in booing and hissing, twirling noisemakers, and stamping their feet.[9]

When we go to church and gather with the body of Christ, we are rejoicing in the truth that God crushed the power of Satan at the cross. The fall of man and the ensuing edict of death has been effectively nullified by the Giver of Life who said,

"I am the resurrection and the life; he who believes in Me shall live, even if he dies" (John 11:25).

We've been delivered from the power of the grave—our death is only the doorway to everlasting life.

And you can be assured that none of the Jews in Persia ever got over the way God miraculously rescued them. I imagine *Purim* was never boring.

And I can imagine how their joy led some of their Persian neighbors to turn in faith as Gentile proselytes to the God of Abraham, Isaac, and Jacob.

Will this be true of your life, as well? Will you make your life a living monument to what Christ has done? Will you contribute joy to your local congregation of believers—as well as the world around you?

Esther and Mordecai understood the importance of remembering God's providential and gracious actions, and we should do the same . . . every day.

Before we roll up the scroll of Esther, let me call attention to two more discoveries from our study.

- **The providence of God reflects His grace . . . it ought to be remembered.**

We often tend to build memorials to remember bad or sorrowful things, don't we? The Enemy of our soul loves to taunt us with past failures, past wrongs, past disappointments, disasters, and calamities which cause us to see our lives as a long dark tunnel with no light at the end.[10]

To counteract the discouragement of past failures and the constant whispering of the Enemy, take time to appreciate and *remember* better times.

Start a journal and make a list of the times you saw God's hand at work in your life, whether great or small. Make a list of your spiritual successes, and then thank the Lord for every one of them.

It occurred to me that monuments were never built in places where Orville and Wilbur Wright *failed* to get airborne. You won't find a granite slab marking all the spots where these brothers crashed either. And there were plenty of places, too.

Remember, the memorial is located where the Wright brothers *flew* . . . everything else, for the most part, has been forgotten.

That's pretty good advice, repeated in the words of the Apostle Paul when he wrote,

> **[F]*orgetting what lies behind and reaching forward to what lies ahead, I press on toward the goal* . . .** (Philippians 3:13*b*-14*a*).

- **The providence of God is spiritually discerned . . . it shouldn't be ignored.**

The last chapter of the Book of Esther isn't a happily-ever-after for everyone. The story wraps up with the king imposing yet another tax on his kingdom, which is another way of saying that things went back to normal— at least, for him.

Tragically, not much changed in his life. There's no conversion to Esther and Mordecai's God; there's no mention of a palace revival. In fact, we know from history that Ahasuerus did little more than build his harem and his palaces before being assassinated in his bedchamber a few years later.

The challenging truth for all of us who claim the God of Esther as our Lord is that we, too, can go about life, living it as usual, and miss out on seeing God's providential hand at work around us.

This is a wake-up call for us to be aware and alert. Don't settle for the world's attitude that coincidences happen and life is just a roll of the dice.

Not a chance.

Whether we see it or not, there is significance in every event and every decision, no matter how mundane. Every step we take is fashioned with purpose as God continues to move us toward His final and ultimate will.

There's actually more to the life of Esther than meets the eye—God wasn't quite finished with her testimony yet.

Upon her husband's death, God raised up one of his sons to take the throne.

Perhaps you remember that one of the young king's most trusted servants came into his presence, his face filled with sadness. When asked about it, the servant delivered a courageous request to the king.

The servant's name was Nehemiah. He had only recently heard that the Jewish people in Jerusalem were being attacked and their reconstruction efforts had been destroyed. He begged the king for permission to return to his homeland and help his people.

The king took pity on him and granted his petition.

There is strong evidence to support the fact that Esther was with the king when Nehemiah made his petition. We're told that the queen was sitting next to the king when Nehemiah made his request *(Nehemiah 2:6)*.

We know from history—and the Book of Esther—that it wasn't customary for the king's favored wife to sit on a throne next to him. The word *queen* in this verse most likely refers to the Queen Mother, who would have been Esther.

Imagine that: Esther's influence continued 21 years after the Book of Esther closed. Her example of aiding the Jewish people was now repeated by the king's court again.

- **The providence of God is physically invisible . . . it's ultimately invincible.**

Here we are at the end of our study and we've come full circle. The study ends *exactly* where it began.

At the end of the book, God is the hero. He alone is deserving of all our praise. The Book of Esther reminds us that God, through the working of His invisible providence, keeps His promises.

God's name is never mentioned once in this story, but those who decide to ignore this book for that reason miss out on incredible truths God left for us to uncover.

Esther is a book for every struggling Christian who can't seem to see God through the fog of life. It's a book for every discouraged Christian who is weighed down by persecution in a world that is so opposed to the Gospel. And it is a book for every forgetful Christian who needs reminding that God cares for His people . . . deeply . . . faithfully.

This is the Gospel according to Esther.

God may be invisible, but He remains invincible.

As Charles Wesley penned it:

Ye servants of God,
Your Master proclaim,
And publish abroad His wonderful name;
The name all-victorious of Jesus extol:
His kingdom is glorious, He rules over all.

ENDNOTES

CHAPTER 1

1   John Blanchard, *Where Is God When Things Go Wrong?* (Evangelical Press, 2005), 5.

2   Ibid, 9.

3   Ibid, 13.

4   Adapted from John MacArthur, "God, Sovereignty, and Evil" (blog posting/July 14, 2008).

5   Blanchard, 31.

6   John C. Whitcomb, *Esther: Triumph of God's Sovereignty* (Moody Press, 1979), 20.

7   Peter A. Steveson, *Ezra, Nehemiah and Esther* (BJU Press, 2011), 210.

8   Debra Reid, *Tyndale Old Testament Commentaries: Esther* (Inter Varsity Press, 2008), 62.

9   Colin D. Jones, *Exploring Esther: Serving the Unseen God* (Day One Publications, 1978), 19.

10   Karen H. Jobes, *The NIV Application Commentary: Esther* (Zondervan, 1999), 28.

11   J. Sidlow Baxter, *Explore the Book* (Zondervan Publishing, 1960), 262.

12   General Editor, John H. Walton, *Zondervan Illustrated Bible Backgrounds Commentary: Esther* (Zondervan, 2009), 397.

13   *Zondervan Illustrated Bible Backgrounds Commentary*, 474.

14   Jones, 10.

CHAPTER 2

1   Karen H. Jobes, *The NIV Application Bible: Esther* (Zondervan, 1999), 21.

2   Bibliotheca Sacra, *The Archaeological Background of Esther*, April-June 1980.

3   J. Vernon McGee, *Esther: The Romance of Providence* (Thomas Nelson, 1982), 7.

4   Ibid, 61.

5   Anthony Tomasino, *Zondervan Illustrated Bible Backgrounds Commentary: Esther* (Zondervan, 2009), 475.

6   Gary V. Smith, *Cornerstone Biblical Commentary: Ezra, Nehemiah, Esther* (Tyndale House Publishers, 2010), 232.

7   Ibid, 231.

8   Colin D. Jones, *Exploring Esther: Serving the Unseen God* (Day One Publications, 1978), 12.

⁹ A. Boyd Luter and Barry C. Davis, *God Behind the Seen: Expositions of the Books of Ruth & Esther* (Baker, 1995), 125.

¹⁰ Cyril J. Barber, *Ezra and Esther* (Wipf & Stock Publishers, 2007), 111.

¹¹ Charles R. Swindoll, quoting Alexander Whyte in *Esther: A Woman of Strength & Dignity* (Word Publishing, 1997), 26.

¹² Ibid, 30.

CHAPTER 3

¹ Cyril J. Barber, *Ezra and Esther* (Wipf & Stock Publishers, 2007), 117.

² Adapted from Peter A. Steveson, *Ezra, Nehemiah, and Esther* (BJU Press, 2011), 206.

³ A. Boyd Luter and Barry C. Davis, *God Behind the Seen: Expositions of the Books of Ruth & Esther* (Baker, 1995).

⁴ Jobes, 94.

⁵ Gary V. Smith, *Cornerstone Biblical Commentary: Ezra, Nehemiah, Esther* (Tyndale House Publishers, 2010), 238.

⁶ Debra Reid, *Tyndale Old Testament Commentaries: Esther* (Tyndale House, 2008), 78.

⁷ Steveson, 226.

⁸ Anthony Tomasino, *Zondervan Illustrated Bible Backgrounds Commentary: Volume 3* (Zondervan, 2009), 485.

⁹ Smith, 239.

¹⁰ Luter and Davis, 155.

¹¹ Colin D. Jones, *Exploring Esther: Serving the Unseen God* (Day One Publications, 2005), 40.

¹² John C. Whitcomb, *Esther: Triumph of God's Sovereignty* (Moody Press, 1979), 50.

CHAPTER 4

¹ Karen H. Jobes, *The NIV Application Commentary: Esther* (Zondervan, 1999), 120.

² Ibid, 118.

³ Debra Reid, *Tyndale Old Testament Commentaries: Esther* (Tyndale House, 2008), 86.

⁴ Jobes, 95.

⁵ Peter A. Steveson, *Ezra, Nehemiah, and Esther* (BJU Press, 2011), 232.

⁶ Jobes, 118.

⁷ Adapted from Colin D. Jones, *Exploring Esther: Serving the Unseen God* (Day One Publications, 2005), 47.

⁸ Steveson, 235.

9   Bayle Roche @searchingquotes.com.

10 J. Vernon McGee, *Esther: The Romance of Providence* (Thomas Nelson, 1982), 64.

11 A. Boyd Luter and Barry C. Davis, *God Behind the Seen: Expositions of the Books of Ruth & Esther* (Baker, 1995), 204.

12 Steveson, 236.

13 Luter and Davis, 207.

14 Knute Larson and Kathy Dahlen, *Holman Old Testament Commentary: Ezra, Nehemiah, Esther* (Holman Publishers, 2005), 311.

15 Erwin Lutzer, *Hitler's Cross* (Moody Press, 1995), 94.

16 Ibid.

17 Ibid, 65.

18 Ibid, 66.

19 Ibid, 144.

CHAPTER 5

1   great-quotes.com/quotes/author/Harriet/Tubman.

2   Ibid.

3   harriettubman.com.

4   Karen H. Jobes, *The NIV Application Commentary: Esther* (Zondervan, 1999), 126.

5   Adapted from Jobes, 233.

6   Peter A. Steveson, *Ezra, Nehemiah, and Esther* (BJU Press, 2011), 241.

7   Charles R. Swindoll, *Esther: A Woman of Strength & Dignity* (Word Publishing, 1997), 79.

8   Anthony Tomasino, *Zondervan Illustrated Bible Backgrounds Commentary: Volume 3* (Zondervan, 2009), 490.

9   John C. Whitcomb, *Everyman's Bible Commentary: Esther: Triumph of God's Sovereignty* (Moody Press, 1979), 74.

10 A. Boyd Luter and Barry C. Davis, *God Behind the Seen: Expositions of the Books of Ruth and Esther* (Baker, 1995), 229.

11 Tomasino, 491.

12 Luter & Davis, 232.

13 Whitcomb, 78.

14 Knute Larson and Kathy Dahlen, *Holman Old Testament Commentary: Ezra, Nehemiah, Esther* (Holman, 2005), 321.

15 Chris Brady, *Rascal: Making a Difference by Becoming an Original Character* (Obstacles Press, 2010), 49.

16 Swindoll, 85.

17 Swindoll, 86.

18 Brady, 33.

19 Quoted in Swindoll, 87.

CHAPTER 6

1 Robert J. Morgan, *Nelson's Complete Book of Stories, Illustrations,& Quotes*, (Thomas Nelson, 2000), 650-653.

2 John C. Whitcomb, *Esther: Triumph of God's Sovereignty* (Moody Press, 1979), 83.

3 Knute Larson and Kathy Dahlen, *Holman Old Testament Commentary: Ezra, Nehemiah, Esther* (Holman Publishers, 2005), 331.

4 Peter A. Steveson, *Ezra, Nehemiah, and Esther* (BJU Press, 2011), 250.

5 Adele Berlin, *The JPS Torah Commentary: Esther* (The Jewish Publication Society, 2001), 59.

6 Karen H. Jobes, *The NIV Application Commentary: Esther* (Zondervan, 1999), 153.

7 Colin D. Jones, *Exploring Esther: Serving the Unseen God* (Day One Publications, 2005), 86.

8 Jobes, 153.

9 Nelson, 603.

CHAPTER 7

1 A. Boyd Luter and Barry C. Davis, *God Behind the Seen: Expositions of the Books of Ruth and Esther* (Baker, 1995), 286.

2 J. Vernon McGee, *Esther: The Romance of Providence* (Thomas Nelson, 1982), 112.

3 Charles R. Swindoll, *Esther: A Woman of Strength & Dignity* (Word Publishing, 1997), 132.

4 Karen H. Jobes, *The NIV Application Commentary: Esther* (Zondervan, 1999), 165.

5 Anthony Tomasino, *Zondervan Illustrated Bible Backgrounds Commentary: Esther* (Zondervan, 2009), 496.

6 Luter and Davis, 296.

7 Jobes, 166.

8 Ravi Zacharias, *Jesus Among Other Gods: The Absolute Claims of the Christian Message* (Zondervan, 2000), 17.

CHAPTER 8

1 Anthony Tomasino, *Zondervan Illustrated Bible Backgrounds Commentary: Volume 3, Esther* (Zondervan, 2009), 480.

[2] John Whitcomb, *Esther: Triumph of God's Sovereignty* (Moody Press, 1979), 42.

[3] Tomasino, 480.

[4] about.usps.com/who-we-are/postal-history/mission-motto.pdf.

[5] Charles R. Swindoll, *Esther: A Woman of Strength & Dignity* (Word Publishing, 1997), 143.

[6] Cyril J. Barber, *Ezra and Esther* (Wipf & Stock Publishers, 2007).

[7] Gary V. Smith, *Cornerstone Biblical Commentary: Ezra, Nehemiah, Esther* (Tyndale House Publishers, 2010), 278.

[8] J. Vernon McGee, *Esther: The Romance of Providence* (Thomas Nelson, 1982), 126.

[9] Barber, 167.

[10] Luter and Davis, 323.

[11] Tomasino, 499.

[12] Karen H. Jobes, *The NIV Application Commentary: Esther* (Zondervan, 1999), 196.

[13] Swindoll, 169.

[14] Swindoll, 163.

CHAPTER 9

[1] Tom Crouch, *The Bishop's Boys* (W.W. Norton & Company, 1989), 12.

[2] Karen H. Jobes, *NIV Application Commentary: Esther* (Zondervan, 1999), 214.

[3] Jobes, p. 220.

[4] W. H. Griffith Thomas Memorial Lectures, November 6-9, 1979 (Bibliotheca Sacra, Dallas Theological Seminary, April-June 1980), 112.

[5] Robert J. Morgan, *Nelson's Complete Book of Stories, Illustrations & Quotes* (Thomas Nelson, 2000), 181.

[6] Jobes, 146.

[7] Ibid, 147.

[8] Jobes, 215.

[9] Knute Larson and Kathy Dahlen, *Holman Old Testament Commentary: Ezra, Nehemiah, Esther* (Holman, 2005), 375.

[10] Swindoll, 175.

SCRIPTURE INDEX